RON CHERNOW

The Death of the Banker

Ron Chernow holds degrees in English literature from Yale and Cambridge universities. His articles on business, politics, and history have appeared in more than forty national and regional publications. His celebrated first book, *The House of Morgan*, won the National Book Award for nonfiction and the Ambassador Award for best book on American culture. *The Warburgs* was awarded the Columbia Business School's 1993 George S. Eccles Prize for Excellence in Economic Writing, and was named a Notable Book by *The New York Times* and one of the year's twelve best nonfiction books by the American Library Association. He lives in Brooklyn with his wife, Valerie, a sociologist.

The Death of the Banker

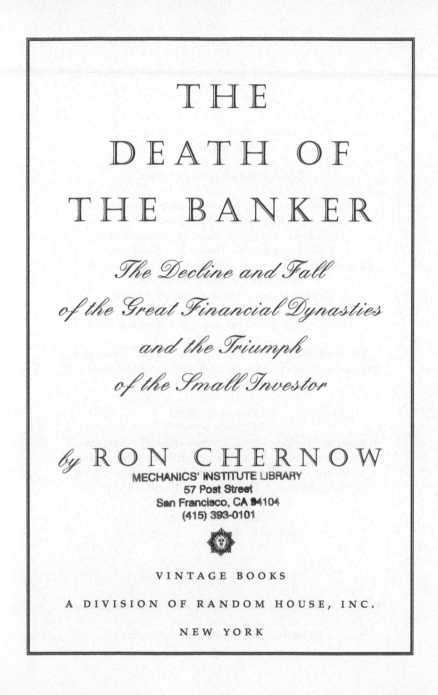

THE

DEATH OF

THE BANKER

The Decline and Fall

of the Great Financial Dynasties

and the Triumph

of the Small Investor

by RON CHERNOW

VINTAGE BOOKS

A DIVISION OF RANDOM HOUSE, INC.

NEW YORK

A VINTAGE ORIGINAL, JULY 1997
FIRST EDITION

Published in the United States by Vintage Books,
a division of Random House, Inc., New York.
Originally published in Canada in somewhat different form
by Vintage Canada, a division of
Random House of Canada Limited, Toronto.

Library of Congress Cataloging in Publication Data
Chernow, Ron.
The death of the banker : the decline and fall of the great
financial dynasties and the triumph of the small investor / by
Ron Chernow.—1st ed.
                p.   cm.
"A Vintage original."
ISBN 978-0-375-70037-8
1. Banks and banking—United States—History—20th century.
2. Trust companies—United States—History—20th century.
3. Finance, Personal—United States.   4. Bankers—United
States.   5. Morgan, J. Pierpont (John Pierpont), 1837-1913.
6. Warburg family.   I. Title.
HG2481.C42   1997
332.1'0973—dc21   97-16318
CIP

Book design by Cathryn S. Aison

Random House Web address: http://www.randomhouse.com/

Printed in the United States of America
20 19 18 17 16 15 14

FOR MY FATHER,

ISRAEL CHERNOW,

WHO HAD THE COURAGE AND QUIET STRENGTH

TO SURVIVE HIS MEDICAL ORDEAL.

CONTENTS

INTRODUCTION

*S*ometimes authors are guilty of such excruciating subtlety that even their most faithful readers fail to spot the themes artfully embedded in their work. Such, I fear, was the case with my two lengthy sagas of banking dynasties, *The House of Morgan* and *The Warburgs*. Some special pleading is in order. Since many people consider "banking" synonymous with "boring," the financial historian is tempted to sugarcoat the pill with diverting tales and thick dollops of local color, sometimes obscuring underlying ideas. Having undertaken to write two plump banking tomes, I tried to keep my touch light in deference to the material's weight. Perhaps novelists picture their readers curling up with their books in a fondly appreciative mood. I see my readers as a moody, bad-tempered crew, stamping their feet and glancing impatiently at their watches. To appease them, I have tried to craft well-paced narratives with enough characters to populate a Dickens novel. Now, with some sense of unfinished business, I welcome the chance to exhume those buried themes.

By design, my banking sagas have spanned more than a century of tumultuous events, for I wanted to depict both the heyday and the twilight of the financial gods. For the past decade, I have been intrigued by the conundrum of why the storied financial dy-

nasties—the Rothschilds, Morgans, Barings, Warburgs et al.—
flared so brilliantly at a certain historic juncture, then fell into
eclipse. Why was their reign so spectacular but brief? These small,
august private banks gave way to financial conglomerates that
still proudly flaunt their predecessors' names and traffic in their
inherited romantic histories as marketing tools; nothing sells
quite so well these days as a classy image. But the dynastic families have long since faded from view, along with the whole web of
intimate relationships with companies and sovereign states that
constituted the essence of their power.

In this trio of essays, I try to explain why the financial dynasties have receded to the status of historic dinosaurs—that is, why
they represent not a permanent feature of economic life but a
fleeting phase in the development of capitalist economies. My aim
isn't to rummage in musty archives and evoke forgotten tycoons
for their antiquated charm. The foremost banking dynasties tell us
much about the shifting constellation of economic and political
power. For this reason, I take their demise as my starting point for
a panoramic survey of the world of high finance during the past
two centuries. For all their majesty, the financial dynasties have
been canaries in the coal mine, telling us much about unseen
forces at work in the capital markets.

The first piece in this book, entitled "The Death of the
Banker," was delivered in Toronto in April 1997 as the Barbara
Frum Memorial Lecture. While the printed version is consider-
ably longer than the spoken one, it expounds the same points,
albeit embellished with more bells and whistles. For future histo-
rians, the salient fact of twentieth-century finance will be the
sharp erosion of banker power—that is, the dwindling role of the
financial intermediary. Bankers are glorified go-betweens, conduits for capital flows. During the twentieth century, they have
progressively yielded power to providers of capital (both retail
and institutional investors), on the one hand, and consumers of
capital (notably large multinational corporations), on the other,

and in the process the banker's intermediary role in the financial equation has declined. A horrid term is sometimes employed to describe this phenomenon—*disintermediation*—but I will try, as much as possible, to avoid all such obfuscatory language and resort to plain English.

Since *banking* is a word subject to many meanings, it might be useful to lodge a caveat here. I am dealing principally with the Olympian world of high finance, what the French call *haute banque*. The reader must banish mundane thoughts of automated tellers, car loans, home mortgages, and so on, and ascend into the upper atmosphere of wholesale finance. This is the tony world that caters to large companies, sovereign states, and "high-net-worth" individuals—once upon a time known as "The Rich."

Many readers will say that I could have avoided unnecessary confusion by calling this book *The Death of the Financier* and that the term *banker* here is a misleading misnomer. Yet I use the word precisely to avoid confusion and facilitate comparisons across time and space. Ever since the Glass-Steagall Act of the 1930s, American finance has been partitioned into commercial banks (which take deposits and make loans) and investment banks (which issue, trade, and distribute securities). Since our discussion shuttles between an old world innocent of such distinctions, and a new world in which this nomenclature applies, "banker" seemed the best catchall term. When I talk of banking in the modern era, I am usually referring to investment bankers, although I wanted the liberty to cite parallel developments in commercial banking. Once again, banking is a conveniently elastic term that can be stretched across a multitude of situations. This is especially true when I turn to Germany, where the system of universal banking never disappeared.

Historically, the denizens of *haute banque* disdained the retail world of small investors and inhabited a separate, rarefied, hermetically sealed universe. The savings of small investors were considered too inconsequential to finance business or government, and they were duly snubbed by the top-hatted money men. During the past generation, the small investor has evolved, in striking fashion, from a bit player and pariah to the mainstay of global financial markets. This shift has been paralleled by a convergence of wholesale and retail finance. Hence, our story originates in a vanished world of paunchy men with watch chains, striped pants, and thick cigars, and ends up with the modern mutual-fund boom. Banded together in mutual funds, the meek have finally inherited the financial earth as the American economy has evolved from one based on banker power to one centered in the stock market.

In reprinting my Barbara Frum Memorial Lecture, Random House of Canada invited me to append two companion pieces. In response, I decided to revisit both *The House of Morgan* and *The Warburgs* in supplementary essays that might serve to extend and illustrate the thesis of my Frum lecture. For those who have read those two sagas, I hope these essays will provide fresh insights and offer more than dehydrated morsels left over from the more ample spread they remember. Since J. Pierpont Morgan appears in the lecture and in the essay of the same name, I apologize to the reader, in advance, for a small amount of unavoidable repetition. Few people can resist the invitation to pontificate before an audience, and I would like to express my profound appreciation to David Frum and his family for giving me my hour to strut and amble upon the lecture stage. I'm also grateful to Doug Pepper of Random House of Canada and Marty Asher of Vintage Books, who provided the editorial enthusiasm that conquers a writer's midnight doubts. As always, I would also like to thank my agent, the indefatigable Melanie Jackson, and my lovely, long-suffering partner in crime, Valerie. My parents continue to provide inspiration by word and deed. Finally, I hope this volume helps to further honor the memory of the late Barbara Frum, one of the true giants of Canadian broadcasting.

The Death of the Banker

The Death of the Banker

1

When I prophesy the death of the banker, I fear that instead of provoking weeping and lamentations, the news will be greeted by the heartless reader with a sigh of relief and loud, prolonged hosannas. For is there any creature on God's green earth so unloved as a banker? We envision him in stereotypical form as a grim, humorless man in late middle age with iron-gray hair, wire-rimmed spectacles, and a costive disposition. Of somber mien, with a permanent scowl on his face, he wears the dark, mono-chromatic suits of a small-town funeral director. In this historical caricature, he seems a born misanthrope who delights in saying no and rebuffing frivolous, unworthy enterprises. He maintains constant vigilance against the fuzzy claims and inflated numbers put forward by mischievous debtors whose principal object in life—or so he is firmly convinced—is to defraud him and bank-rupt his institution.

If the banker, traditionally, took this jaundiced view of human nature, it was because his assigned function in the financial cos-mos was to ration scarce credit. Dispensing something rare and precious, he was perpetually on the defensive and had to be far more adept at spurning prospective borrowers than gratifying their fond wishes. But money has now become a banal commodity, available everywhere at the touch of a button or the flick of a computer switch. Money is, literally, everywhere. Automated teller machines line the streets, shopping malls, and airports, as if they were vending machines selling soda, candy, or cigarettes. Retired baseball players hawk home-equity loans in television commercials and solicitations for new credit cards come cascading in with each day's mail. (Even sinners who have filed for personal bankruptcy are instantly absolved by the financial priesthood and tenderly welcomed back into the fold.) We inhabit an age of superabundant credit and its purveyors, as with any other product manufactured in surplus, must advertise heavily to stimulate demand and soak up existing supply.

In this essay, I plan to meditate upon the metamorphosis of the banker in the twentieth century, from the Spartan age of limited capital to our own hedonistic age of bountiful cash. I'm going to consider, in particular, the rise and fall of the great banking dynasties, the financial overlords of the nineteenth and early twentieth centuries, and carry the story through to the unexpected triumph of the small mutual-fund investor, the implausible tycoon of the late twentieth century. When I talk of "The Death of the Banker," the reader shouldn't picture the sallow, overworked teller at the corner bank, the one accustomed to moving in slow motion when he's in a rush, but rather someone more likely to sport red suspenders and Gucci loafers and waggle thick Cuban cigars. Yes, I'm referring to those people who take home obnoxious salaries, whose Christmas bonuses dwarf not just our annual salary, but our entire net worth, and who sometimes seem immune from normal human misery. These bankers scarcely seem crucified by recent financial developments. So how can I possibly suggest that this charmed breed, the darlings of the business media, belong to an endangered species? Don't we live in an age that fairly rings with the razzle-dazzle of big deals, the babble about megamergers, the omnipresence of the stock market in our culture? Aren't these people—if the truth be told—much too powerful?

Once upon a time, I was also impressed by the power and wealth of these youthful wheeler-dealers. Then, as I burrowed into my research for *The House of Morgan*, I began to dust off and resurrect the forgotten world of the fin de siècle bankers. Here I discovered sleek tycoons who held undisputed sway over transcontinental railroads, industrial trusts, investment houses, and estates the size of small duchies. They boasted yachts as big as battleships, smoked cigars as thick as small torpedoes, and treated presidents and prime ministers as peers—sometimes even condescended to them as the sovereigns of struggling, inferior states. These men seemed to stand at the pinnacle, not just of the financial world, but of society.

For those few who have not read *The House of Morgan* cover to cover and committed it to memory, let me briefly evoke the incomparable splendor of Mr. J. Pierpont Morgan (1837–1913), the senior partner of J.P. Morgan & Company, who was endowed with the nickname "Jupiter" on Wall Street. At the zenith of his splendor, Mr. Morgan controlled one-third of America's railroads, and this at a time when railroads comprised 60 percent of all the stocks on the New York Stock Exchange and nineteen of the twenty most actively traded bonds were railroad instruments. After the 1901 creation of U.S. Steel, the first billion-dollar corporation, he controlled about 70 percent of the steel industry and figured largely in the affairs of the three leading insurance companies. Besides the Morgan bank, he reigned over Bankers Trust and Guaranty Trust (later folded into the Morgan bank) and held major stakes in the banks that became Chase and Citicorp. When Morgan made the offhand remark "America is good enough for me," *The Commoner*, the newspaper of populist William Jennings

Bryan, was quick to retort, "Whenever you're tired of it, you can give it back." That was the popular image of J. P. Morgan—the harsh, flinty landlord of the United States, exacting his mite from every American. The reader will begin to see what I mean when I say that even the richest deal-makers and most overweening yuppies of today seem small and bland mortals beside a colossus such as Morgan.

As I excavated the Morgan archives, I was forced to ask myself, how could a single individual amass such power? And why did it seem inconceivable that a contemporary financier could attain even a fraction of that fabled power? To elucidate this mystery, I spent a lot of time digging through dusty documents, blackening my hands with ancient soot, but I also engaged in a fair bit of daydreaming. Wandering around Wall Street or the London financial district, the City, I was intrigued by the old, private banking houses—those impenetrable fortresses with thick walls and heavily draped windows, steeped in their own gloomy dignity and majesty. These historic buildings shared a tell-tale feature that intrigued me—they posted no nameplate, as if unwilling to divulge their identity to bemused pedestrians. At the corner of Broad and Wall in lower Manhattan, the elegantly chiselled, marble headquarters of J.P. Morgan & Company posted the number 23 on the door and nothing else. This haughty reticence stood out in a land of hucksterism and high-pressure salesmanship, where businessmen seldom balk at trumpeting their presence. Why did these wholesale banks so brazenly defy the curious? Why did they wreathe themselves in unfathomable mystery? What kind of business shrank from public view? Everyone remembers the famous "Rosebud" riddle in the movie *Citizen Kane*—the inscrutable last word, croaked out by the dying Kane, that is the movie's central enigma. For me, the absence of nameplates on those old banking houses seemed the clue that might pry open the secret of how Morgan had gathered such immense power.

Before embarking on a tour of some financial dynasties, I must pause and—at the risk of becoming a pedantic bore—burden the reader with an interpretive framework. So many different kinds of banking systems populate the financial bestiary that I needed some universal yardstick for comparing them. My solution has been to picture any financial system as represented by a simple graph with three bars. As the middleman, the eternal matchmaker, the wholesale banker naturally occupies the center position. He is forever suspended between the providers of capital—whether individual or institutional investors—and the consumers of capital—whether individual, business, or governmental borrowers. Any financial system, no matter how intricate, can be reduced to this crude, simplistic framework.

Now, to gauge the changing strength of the banker, we cannot simply appraise the scope of his activities or the scale of his capital—the absolute standard applied daily in the business press. Rather, the banker's true power in any period depends upon his relative strength compared with that of the providers and consumers of capital. To take a commonplace example: in negotiating an offering of stocks and bonds, which party has the upper hand—the company issuing the securities, the banker underwriting it, or the investor absorbing it? As we make our long, winding, eventful excursion through financial history, the reader should try to keep that three-bar graph before his mind's eye—the provider of capital, the banking intermediary, and the consumer of capital. Over time, you will see some surprising changes, and in time you may understand my announced requiem for the banker. Now, armed with our analytic tool, let us set off on our journey.

2

$\mathcal{I}$t is a common adage in the financial world that money begets money, that money—in the archaic sense of the word—is prolific. In the last analysis, even the greatest bankers are perhaps no more than brilliant tricksters, puffed up with other people's money. Many would-be tycoons cherish the fancy that, if only some kindly stranger would come along and give them a sufficiently large endowment, they could inaugurate their own financial dynasty. So perhaps we should commence our tour with the fundamental question of how the leading financial dynasties obtained that all-important grubstake that first propelled them down the yellow brick road to riches.

Let us start *ab ovo*. In the obscure dawn of high finance, banking was a mere by-product of the world of trade and took a long time to evolve into a discrete profession, consecrated by legal authorities with protective charters. Commodity merchants often advanced farmers money against crop deliveries or extended loans against the security of merchandise left for safekeeping. That many toplofty London banks still style themselves as "merchant banks" testifies to these distant origins. In fact, the illustrious merchant banks of the nineteenth century, besides brokering and discounting bills, traded commodities on their own account and chartered and insured ships, sending argosies to distant ports. The natural progression from commerce to finance is worth mentioning here for it left open the intriguing possibility that clients of merchant banks with surplus, lendable funds might someday become rival banks themselves. As we have seen repeatedly in our own day, any successful business that engenders a large surplus is, potentially, an embryonic bank. In the absence of special regulatory restrictions, banking seems to spring spontaneously from other forms of economic activity.

Even the Rothschilds, those counting-house wizards, couldn't manufacture money from thin air and had to find seed money. Recently the Israeli historian Amos Elon published the first biography of the original Rothschild patriarch, Mayer Amschel Rothschild. It was he who sired the five gifted sons who fanned out across Europe and forged interlocking partnerships in Frankfurt, London, Paris, Vienna, and Naples—a gilded diaspora celebrated by the five intertwined arrows of the family insignia. Operating from the sunless gloom and formidable stench of the Frankfurt ghetto, this first Rothschild was a resourceful businessman who dealt in rare coins and medals, antiques and curios, clothing, flour, and second-hand goods. Only slowly did his banking business emerge from this chaotic assemblage of businesses. In fact, banking didn't predominate in his varied product mix until 1810, two years before his death. The profits extracted from these diversified activities could never have provided the capital for a first-rate banking house. So where did Rothschild get the money to become, well, a Rothschild?

A century later, industrial enterprises would generate surplus capital, the sine qua non of any modern banking system, but at this more primitive stage of capitalist development, the taxing power of a despot was one of the few means to that end. Mayer Amschel found it necessary to grovel before the local nobleman, Wilhelm IX, the landgrave of Hesse and the heir to an enormous fortune who was—luckily for Rothschild—an avid coin collector. The landgrave's imagination was fertile in figuring out ways to extort money from his hapless subjects. For instance, legend claims that every time he fathered another illegitimate child, he raised the salt tax so that mistress and love child could live in royal comfort. Since Wilhelm broadcast his seed liberally throughout the realm and could have single-handedly stocked a small orphanage—the size of his illegitimate brood ran as high as seventy children, according to one count—the populace constantly reeled from a sky-high salt tax. Devising new torments for his subjects, Wilhelm also auctioned off Hessian mercenaries to George III of England to suppress the American Revolution. If you're curious about the grisly arithmetic of cannon-fodder, Wilhelm charged fifty-one thaler per foot soldier and collected the same amount for each one killed in battle—presumably since each death deprived him of income from future sales; three wounded soldiers equaled one dead man, and also fetched fifty-one thaler. Not a sweet-smelling fortune.

As a man who needed to command a large pool of capital, Mayer Amschel had no choice but to bow and scrape before this fickle sovereign. His letters to the landgrave reek with obsequious flattery, the shameless application of honorific titles that was de rigueur for courtiers in those days; the ambitious banker needed cloying adjectival artistry no less than a quick mind for numbers. With his decided flair for secrecy and intrigue, Rothschild undertook numerous confidential missions for the landgrave. When Wilhelm was driven into exile by his refusal to join Napoleon's Confederation of the Rhine, Rothschild helped him to outwit the French occupation troops by hiding some of his patron's securities in his house, a place punctuated with more trapdoors, sliding panels, and secret compartments than a magician's trunk. Even Rothschild's carriage was honeycombed with hidden places to squirrel away money. Ultimately, Rothschild was rewarded with a near monopoly on negotiating the numerous and highly lucrative state loans issued by Wilhelm.

From the perspective of two centuries, one is struck that this first Rothschild was so purely a creature of court intrigues, lacked corporate clients in his banking business, and seemed to engage almost exclusively in affairs of state. Nervous, insecure—an anxiety exacerbated by his precarious status as a Jew—he could only bask in the reflected glory of the landgrave and had to be extremely submissive, even sycophantic, to retain royal favor. A proud man who had to endure unending snubs and neglectful treatment in silence, he suffered from the lopsided nature of his power relationship with his sovereign. Let us glance for a moment at our bar graph: at this point in history, the power of the capital provider, Wilhelm IX, was infinitely greater than that of his agent, Rothschild, who could be snuffed out by an impatient grunt or pained grimace from his princely master. As for the consumers of Wilhelm's capital—the impoverished European noblemen who badgered him for loans—they had extremely circumscribed bargaining power in an era marked by a shortage of capital and chartered banks.

I would like to leapfrog ahead to the nineteenth century to provide some vignettes that demonstrate the exalted place in European society that the Rothschilds soon attained. In the early 1840s, the German poet Heinrich Heine visited James de Rothschild in his Parisian office so that he could watch supplicants crook the knee and tug the forelock before the regal banker. According to Heine, potential clients fawned before Rothschild in so many contorted forms that this "wriggling and twisting of the backbone" would have been difficult "for even the best of acrobats." One day he observed a Rothschild servant bearing a chamber pot down the corridor and noted that a stock market speculator instinctively removed his hat in respect as the Rothschild waste passed by. Heine was convinced that any man with so little self-respect would surely end up a millionaire.

Even heads of state would shortly truckle to the Rothschilds. During the Franco-Prussian War, the Prussians laid siege to Paris for nearly four months. During this dreadful time, desperate Parisians butchered zoo animals for meat and supped on assorted cats and rats. Determined to wait out the savagery in comfort, Kaiser Wilhelm, Chancellor Otto von Bismarck, and General Helmuth von Moltke retreated to the Rothschild château at Ferrières. Even the Kaiser was dazzled as he roamed around this vast domain, confiding, "Only a Rothschild could own all that." Bismarck, who spent many pleasant hours blasting Rothschild pheasants from the sky, was eager to wash down this tasty game with the owner's wine. When he questioned the caretaker—a retainer of the old school who would have submitted to the most exquisite torture rather than betray his master—he said that the estate did not contain a single bottle of wine. Bismarck, who was in France after all, was doubtful. After some prodding, the caretaker retracted his statement and admitted to having 100 bottles of Bordeaux in stock. When a still skeptical Bismarck demanded a search of the premises, his troops discovered 17,000 bottles in the cellar. Irate, Bismarck threatened to torch the whole place, then decided it was far wiser to sit down and savor the cache of wine. Within less than a century, the Rothschilds, once the officious servants of monarchs, had grown to be their equal, able to thumb their noses at the Kaiser, Bismarck, and other such minor luminaries on the European scene.

3

*W*hat had changed that allowed the Rothschilds to hurl insults and thunderbolts so freely and treat the loftiest politicos with undisguised condescension? How had they crept out from under the awful, oppressive shadow of local sovereigns to stand forth as unrivaled magnificos in their own right? The plight of the landgrave of Hesse, we should note, was an atypical case of a ruler swimming in surplus cash and urgently needing a banker to invest it. By allowing Rothschild to lend this money circumspectly, off in the wings, the landgrave could obtain the maximum return without ruffling the feathers of patrician relatives who might have naively expected preferential terms. Unencumbered by the baggage of royal feuds, the private banker could obey a strict economic calculus and ignore political distractions. If trouble arose, the ruler could always throw up his hands in mock horror and feigned impotence and disclaim all knowledge of the rash actions of his headstrong banker.

With our vision sharpened by hindsight, we know that the nation-state was predestined to have a ravenous appetite for money. Whether to prosecute wars, spur economic growth, or sprinkle welfare benefits among the citizenry like the tooth fairy, the cash requirements of sovereign states would grow exponentially with time. If you flip through the history of any great banking family, you will invariably find episodes in which they daringly raised money for some cash-strapped government, debilitated by war; or sold horses, uniforms, and other supplies to their armies; or helped to retire an onerous indemnity, imposed by a vindictive, victorious foreign power. It comes as no surprise to learn that government arrangements for spending money raced far ahead of those for raising it, reflecting the superior fun and political utility of the former pursuit. In the nineteenth century, politicians hadn't yet experienced the addictive charms of income taxes or deficit spending, nor did they have subservient central banks with printing presses ready to crank out crisp bills. Of course, rulers could auction off citizens for slaughter in foreign wars or impose punitive excise taxes, like the landgrave of Hesse. But everybody recalled the French Revolution and the capital punishment contrived by Dr. Guillotin, and democracy's spread in the nineteenth century tended to curb such exploitation. Also the finance ministries of the time were notoriously corrupt and inefficient. So when it came to unpopular causes, it often seemed safer and more economical for rulers to promote them with borrowed money rather than to risk a popular backlash. The private banker was a backdoor treasury that allowed sovereigns and politicians to bypass public control.

During the first half of the nineteenth century, great capital aggregations were rare and the House of Rothschild often vied with only a single serious competitor in the field of state finance: Baring Brothers. Of the leading dynasties, the Barings probably had the least color, swagger, or panache. If thorough, prudent citizens of the City of London, they were no less formidable for all that. For centuries the family had resided in North Germany, hard by the Hanseatic cities of Hamburg and Bremen, before the first expatriate Baring moved to England and took up the wool trade in Exeter. When Francis Baring set up shop in London in the mid-eighteenth century, it was not to become a banker, but to broker the family wool shipments from the West Country. Like the first Rothschild, Baring didn't aspire to be a banker but unwittingly mutated into one as an outgrowth of his thriving mercantile business. As he financed consignments of everything from copper to diamonds, he woke up one day to discover that he was, presto, a banker malgré lui.

In leafing through Philip Ziegler's fine history of the family, I was again struck by the nearly complete absence of corporate clients in the early Barings history. During the American Revolution, the firm raised money for the British government, netting a tidy profit. By the mid-nineteenth century, it served as London agent for a select clientele, including the governments of Russia, Norway, Austria, Chile, Argentina, Australia, and the United States. At the time, London was the fountainhead of Canadian capital, and Barings also numbered Canada, Nova Scotia, and New Brunswick among its clients. Whether Barings was carrying out a foreign policy or simply a business transaction was never clear, so intertwined were financial matters with affairs of state.

The Rothschilds, seemingly infallible, committed one fatal lapse of judgment: they discounted the future potential of that rowdy, debt-happy, uncouth country called the United States. Had they set up a Wall Street bank in the nineteenth century, their name today might not have such a musty, antique ring. Barings had no qualms about capitalizing on this misstep, even though they had provided George III with funds to pound those same fractious colonists back into submission. In 1803, all apparently forgiven on the American side, Barings, aided by Hope & Company of Amsterdam, bankrolled the Louisiana Purchase from France—surely the granddaddy of real estate deals—an operation that turned Barings into a trusted confidant of the U.S. government. During the War of 1812, Barings doled out interest to London holders of American bonds, even though money from America had temporarily dried up. With amazing tolerance and solicitude for their bankers, the British government issued no complaint about such heroic service on behalf of the enemy.

During the first half of the nineteenth century, presidents and prime ministers, kings and princes, truckled to the financial grandees of the Rothschild and Baring banks. While not a paid publicist for Barings, the Duc de Richelieu, prime minister under Louis XVIII, might as well have been. He offered an encomium to Barings so eloquent that, had television then existed, it could have formed the basis for a splendid advertising campaign. "There are six great powers in Europe," he said: "England, France, Prussia, Austria, Russia, and Baring Brothers." Like many celebrated comments in history, it is fiendishly difficult to pin down exactly when or where or even if it was said. No matter: the statement, if apocryphal, is much too good to sacrifice. Barings seemed to inspire a veritable cottage industry of writers who penned sweeping tributes to its powers. In 1823, Nicholas Biddle, the president of the Bank of the United States, came up with this lovely couplet: "I prefer my last letter from Barings or Hope / To the finest epistles of Pliny and Pope." Lord Byron burnished the Barings image in a nasty anti-Semitic quatrain that told of the bank's power in disparaging terms:

Who keep[s] the world both old and new, in pain
Or pleasure? Who make[s] politics run glibber all?
The shade of Buonaparte's double daring?
Jew Rothschild and his fellow, Christian Baring.

If you imagine that only poets grew giddy before the Barings'
throne, consider this euphoric diary entry from Swinton Holland,
a Liverpool merchant invited to become a partner of the bank in
December 1814. Had he received a sudden visitation from the
archangel Gabriel, he could not have seemed more exhilarated or
overjoyed by his good fortune. "Omnipotent Ruler of the Universe," he wrote to God, "may I be grateful to thee, for this mark
of thy goodness in elevating my situation in Life."

   If such literary testimonials are any proof, this period represented the apogee of banker power vis-à-vis the state. If you took
the quotation from the Duc de Richelieu and substituted the name
of any modern financial house, even a Goldman, Sachs or a J.P.
Morgan & Co., it would, of course, sound risible. To refer back to
our bar graph, the wholesale banker towered, for the moment,
above government borrowers. Having said that, one can legiti-
mately wonder whether banks were actually so strong or the new
nation-states so weak. After the Civil War, the standing of Baring
Brothers plummeted in the United States, which to some degree
mirrored Washington's decision to recruit a phalanx of home-
grown bankers, ranging from Jay Cooke to J. P. Morgan, to handle
major financial transactions. Of greater moment was the fact that
between the start of the Civil War and the First World War, the
United States introduced a uniform national currency, created the
Federal Reserve System, and initiated a federal income tax.
Equipped with these powers, the nation-state became far more
autonomous in financial matters and far less reliant on the whims
of wholesale bankers.

Just as Baring Brothers' ascendancy in sovereign lending started to wane, a new phase in high finance unfolded to take up the slack: railroad financing. When the first railway boom hit England in the 1840s, the merchant banks didn't exactly distinguish themselves with their strategic foresight. To be more precise, they cravenly ran for cover. Most shrank from getting entangled with this expensive, newfangled technology, a fact noted by Benjamin Disraeli with palpable exasperation: "The mighty loan-mongers, on whose fiat the fate of kings and empires sometimes depended, seemed like men who, witnessing some eccentricity of nature, watched it with mixed feelings of curiosity and alarm." In the end, no self-respecting banker could resist this trend, given the railroads' insatiable need for capital and the rich, mouthwatering returns on investment. In 1845 the French and British Rothschilds cooperated to launch the Chemin de Fer du Nord. By the 1870s and 1880s, the majority of American loans marketed in London were for railroads, and even the reluctant Barings temporarily surpassed Morgan in this area.

For most of the nineteenth century, London merchant banks were in very bad odor among British industrialists, who incessantly carped about the City neglecting them in favor of railways, canals, waterworks, and other capital projects in North and South America. The City banker always seemed more drawn to sweltering jungles or desert ventures than, say, to a Midlands' factory. This situation began to change in America and Britain in the late nineteenth century. As industrial firms expanded, exploiting new economies of scale and serving new global markets, their capital needs exhausted the meager resources available at local banks. To convert the latent value of their companies into cash and perpetuate their firms, founding families had to swallow their pride, surrender control, and sell shares to the public.

In 1886, Sir Edward Guinness of the brewing clan decided to float—the verb seems oddly appropriate here—his business as a public company. For Lord Rothschild, such stock promotion was still vulgar and déclassé, and he turned Guinness down flat, but Thomas Baring retained no such scruples. When Barings opened the Guinness offering to public subscription in October 1886, it exposed the contours of a giant new investing public, famished for such issues. Though police cordoned off the bank, they had difficulty tranquilizing the frenzied mob of applicants. As one newspaper reported, "Special policemen kept back the pushing crowd of clerks, agents, messengers and City men, and pains were taken to have one of the swing doors only partly open, so that none but spectral clerks and Stock Exchange men of the Cassius cut could squeeze in." Some of the desperate tied applications around stones and lobbed them, like so many grenades, through open windows. In the end, the share demand was twenty times greater than the supply, creating not a few bruised feelings among the rejected. People were especially outraged to learn that Barings had reserved more than a quarter of the stock for itself and its partners; once thick tranches were sliced off for the Rothschilds, Morgans, and Hambros, scarcely more than a quarter of the shares were left for the irate general public.

Financial history was actually turning on a hinge here, for, in the massive conversion of closely held companies into publicly owned ones, bankers tucked away big blocks of stock for themselves. They had a sound rationale for doing so: by becoming large shareholders in client companies, they could, in theory, provide reassurance to frazzled investors that companies would be competently managed, and dividend and interest payments would be made in timely fashion. But there was also plenty of potential for abuse with such captive companies. Would bankers safeguard the interests of investors at the expense of the company? Or would they feather their own nests at the expense of both? It was in their close, incestuous dealings with companies that bankers would encounter their most damaging political controversy.

What constituted a salutary distance between a company and its banker would remain a vexed issue, one that still haunts us today as America debates whether to lower the barriers that segregate banking from commerce. Perhaps at this point in our perambulation, we should duck into that discreet building at the corner of Broad and Wall, the one with the understated number 23 on the door. Yes, the building with no nameplate.

4

*M*ore than eighty years after his death, John Pierpont Morgan continues to define our image of the tycoon as a big-bellied man, top-hatted and frock-coated, a fierce, swaggering buccaneer. Here was a big-time financier as P. T. Barnum might have conceived him, with a thunderous voice and a daggerlike gaze, a portly man of vivid appearance and kaleidoscopic moods. On the street, he wielded a cane that might become an instrument of public relations if he wished to go mano a mano with an overly importunate photographer. With a murderous glint in his eye, Morgan would lift his club and wave it until the unwanted intruder disappeared. Clearly no Milquetoast, he felt no need for a public-relations man. He epitomized the high-testosterone tycoon, blessed with a lusty appetite for big deals, big boats, and big, bosomy women. If there was a high point of banker power in American financial history, J. Pierpont Morgan certainly incarnated it.

Later on, I shall have much more to say about the life and times of this outsize personality, but I would like to focus more narrowly here on our evolving theme of the banker, locked in his eternal triangular struggle with investors and borrowers. While "Morgan, Morgan, the Great Financial Gorgon" (as he was skewered in a contemporary stage play) may linger in our memory as the red-blooded, all-American tycoon, his image among coevals was quite different. Brought up in Hartford and Boston, he had an international education unusual for a boy in provincial nineteenth-century America. Around mid-century, his father, Junius Spencer Morgan, was invited to become the junior (later the senior) partner of a distinguished London bank founded by an American expatriate, George Peabody. Hence, Pierpont spent time at a Swiss boarding school on Lake Geneva, and at the University of Göttingen in Germany. He also dallied in London with his family, developing intense affection for the British. England was then the world's banker, the citadel of financial respectability, so that such an upbringing would be immensely useful to the boy. Indeed, by the time Junius Spencer Morgan posted his twenty-year-old son to Wall Street as his agent in 1857, Pierpont was an Anglo-American hybrid. Outwardly, he had the rough swagger and high spirits of a young American male, but he had already internalized much of the dismay with which the British viewed American business practices.

As I have already stressed, finance springs naturally from successful commerce. In the nineteenth century, England was one of the few nations that had attained the level of prosperity that spawns surplus capital, which spills, in turn, across national boundaries in search of the highest return. For British investors, America was a richly tempting "Third World" country, one loaded with pitfalls and with a boorish habit of defaulting on debts; perhaps Mexico or Brazil might serve as a contemporary analogy. In the 1840s, the rogues' gallery of sovereign deadbeats included Pennsylvania, Maryland, and other U.S. states. (The most renegade offender, Mississippi, later went so far as to pass a state constitutional amendment prohibiting repayment of its bonds.) Faced with such recalcitrance, many European investors ruled America off-limits to further investing. When Washington dispatched U.S. Treasury agents to solicit a loan from Baron James de Rothschild in Paris in 1842, the banker brusquely expelled these aliens from his office: "Tell them you have seen the man who is at the head of the finances of Europe, and that he has told you that they cannot borrow a dollar. Not a dollar." One disgruntled London investor, clergyman Sydney Smith, was convinced that America had now degenerated into outright barbarism. Whenever he met a Pennsylvanian at a London dinner, he said, he felt "a disposition to seize and divide him. . . . How such a man can set himself down at an English table without feeling that he owes two or three pounds to every man in the company, I am at a loss to conceive; he has no more right to eat with honest men than a leper has to eat with clean men."

The ostracism didn't last long. Seduced by lush returns on American railroad securities, British investors turned out to have short memories, forgiving natures, and open wallets. American railroads required massive amounts of capital, the British had plenty to lend, and J. Pierpont Morgan would ride herd for these skittish investors. The British welcomed an American railway czar who might save them from the numerous swindlers and fast-talkers. They often had only the haziest picture of where the railroads actually ran, with one contemporary map of the United States showing a baffling blank in mid-continent labeled "The American Desert." Worst of all, the railroads were poorly managed. After the Civil War, helter-skelter growth led to excess trackage, bloated debt, and often ruinous competition. Saddled with surplus capacity, the roads engaged in recurring price wars, which reduced profits and made it hard to pay off bondholders. Dismayed by such distant mayhem, their first contact with cowboy capitalism, the London investors craved an enforcer on the ground who could knock sense into the railroad chieftains and inculcate a sense of responsibility.

With his gaze full of sadness and fiery indignation, Pierpont Morgan offered himself as just such a savior. He felt genuine moral outrage at the railroads' business practices and when deal-

ing with them would always betray something of the stern disci-
plinarian, spanking unruly schoolchildren for their own good.
Early in his career, he mostly represented British creditors to
American borrowers, though the situation reversed itself later on.
According to a favorite Wall Street gag, aboard his yacht, the *Corsair*, Morgan flew the Union Jack over the Stars and Stripes and
the Jolly Roger above them both. For legions of populist critics,
this joke spelled out their enduring image of J. P. Morgan—the
pirate in the pay of British gold.

When Morgan died in 1913, the newspapers listed his estate
as worth $68.3 million (excluding the $50 million worth of art he
had collected), an amount, all told, that would be well in excess of
a billion dollars today. When a startled Andrew Carnegie read
these figures, he pitied poor Morgan. "And to think he was not a
rich man," he said with a sigh. The inadvertent comedy here -
shouldn't obscure a faint trace of truth in Carnegie's lament. As
the journalist John Moody once observed, Morgan's power
stemmed, not from the millions he owned, but from the billions
he commanded. At a time when pockets of capital were small,
few, and widely scattered, he managed to weld them together into
a machinery that could finance large-scale industry.

As the mouthpiece for masses of distant investors, Morgan not
only financed many railroads, but staked out a role as a trusted ar-
biter among them. Railroads are natural monopolies—few routes
can support more than one road—yet they operated after the Civil
War in a rip-roaring, hypercompetitive environment. People would
lay "blackmail" railroads parallel to existing lines solely to extort
bribes for abandoning the new lines. Nowadays we tend to think
of "competition" as a matter of offering superior products at
lower prices. For the cynical, hard-bitten capitalists of the late nineteenth century, operating free of antitrust laws, competition often
meant blatantly rigging markets in their favor and to their rivals'
detriment. For such bold adventurers, market share wasn't won

in the marketplace, but was wrung from rivals behind closed doors. In these days before trade associations, the Morgan bank provided a private, intimate meeting-ground for such negotiations.

Let us contemplate Morgan for a moment, in all his imperial splendor, aboard the *Corsair* on a steamy July morning in the year of our Lord 1885. As his 165-foot, black-hulled steam yacht glides up and down the Hudson River, Morgan sits on deck beneath a striped awning, adding appreciably to New York's air pollution as he puffs a gargantuan cigar. On some days, Morgan would smuggle mistresses aboard the *Corsair*, which became a floating bordello, but on this particular afternoon it was more like a floating conspiracy in restraint of trade. His three sailing companions were Chauncey M. Depew, president of the New York Central Railroad, and George H. Roberts and Frank Thomson, president and vice president of the Pennsylvania Railroad. Evidently with the secret connivance of the Pennsylvania, the West Shore Railroad had constructed a line running up the west shore of the Hudson River—a threat to the New York Central line on the east shore. In reprisal, the New York Central broke ground on a South Pennsylvania road to span the state from Philadelphia to Pittsburgh, taking direct aim at the Pennsylvania Railroad. Employing a favorite tactic, Morgan wouldn't let his yacht return to shore until these railroad adversaries had come to terms. As the *Corsair* sailed up and down the Hudson, Morgan hammered out a quid pro quo by which the West Shore would be scrapped if the new South Pennsylvania line were terminated.

While Morgan was a past master of persuasion, he yearned to exercise more direct control over these endlessly squabbling roads. In the late 1880s, he made vain efforts to cobble together railroad cartels that would prohibit price-cutting and other destructive methods. The failure of these forays primed him for a new tactic when scores of railroads went bankrupt after the 1893 Panic. In reorganizing railroads (or "remorganizing" as wags

would have it), Morgan slimmed down their fixed costs and issued new bonds with lower interest rates, while simultaneously
pacifying investors with ironclad liens on the railroads' land and
mineral holdings. Dispensing with the quiet persuasion of the
past, he decided to create "voting trusts" to run the railroads—
"voting trust" being a polite euphemism for Morgan and a clique
of three or four cronies who would run the road for a five-year period. In transferring such power to Morgan, railroads also paid
him tribute in the form of million-dollar fees. Through this
process, a third of America's railroads fell under J. P. Morgan's
sway. He was never expert in the technical aspects of the roads—
he could probably tell a locomotive from a caboose, but not much
more—but he had partners extremely well versed in such matters.
One such prodigy, Charles Coster, a pale, anxious man unknown
to the general public, sat on the boards of no fewer than fifty-nine
corporations.

Let us stop for another glance at our tripartite financial
model. Remote from the scene, the capital providers, the London
investors, had ceded much of their power to the banker, Pierpont
Morgan, who now acted as their fire-breathing, head-knocking
proxy. On the other side of the equation, many bankrupt railroads
had yielded their autonomy and ended up as wards of the banker.
If we picture the three bars of the graph again, the middle graph
now soars incontestably above the other two. We have arrived at
the apotheosis of the banker, who has benefited from a temporary
imbalance of power in his dealings with the consumers of capital.
We have arrived, in short, at the age of finance capitalism.

With his resources fortified by the railroad reorganizations,
Morgan was ready to act as catalyst for the new industrial trusts.
Presiding over an empire of interlocking partnerships in New
York, Philadelphia, London, and Paris, he could tap pools of cap-
ital, both at home and abroad, and finance megamergers on a
scale hitherto deemed unimaginable. Before the 1890s, American

entrepreneurs had principally relied on wealthy investors and local banks for capital. Now, toward the century's end, American industry was generating surplus capital and emancipating Morgan and other Wall Street bankers from foreign dependence. The capstone of the resulting merger movement was the 1901 creation of U.S. Steel, the first billion-dollar corporation, which Morgan followed up the next year with the formation of International Harvester, the farm-equipment trust.

Many companies involved in these amalgamations were still run by the original entrepreneurs who wanted to sell out to realize the value latent in their companies. Often self-made men who had once worked with their hands, they had a healthy suspicion of financiers, lawyers, accountants, and other educated types who pushed paper and lived by the ledger books. Since many had been coldly rebuffed by bankers early in their careers, they generally didn't relish dealing with the likes of Morgan. But they knew that in order to integrate their companies vertically, achieve economies of scale, and compete in global markets, they had to merge with competitors. With many companies still privately held, it was impossible to use the stock exchange as a mechanism to effect the trusts. And what was needed to consolidate an entire industry far exceeded the paltry capital available in the vaults of small-town banks. Hence, businessmen who had solemnly sworn that they would never submit to that dreaded beast, Wall Street, flocked in numbers to the offices of J.P. Morgan & Company.

As local companies sought national markets for their securities, they needed the imprimatur of a Wall Street banker. Before 1906, for instance, Kidder, Peabody marketed the bonds of American Telephone & Telegraph in the New England area. When the company decided to cultivate a national investing public, it dissolved its links with the Boston-based Kidder and struck an alliance with J.P. Morgan & Company. The Morgan financing enabled the firm to fend off a spirited challenge from independent phone companies and restore its original monopoly status. Nowadays, multinational corporations are often larger, better known, and even better capitalized than their bankers. In the early 1900s, by contrast, many of these companies were local and far less prominent than their Wall Street bankers. The main thing that a Morgan could confer upon a fledgling company was not so much his capital as his cachet, his signal to jittery investors that they could safely invest their money in this little-known firm.

In this situation, J. P. Morgan and his financial peers were in a position to extract highly advantageous terms from clients. The same way that Morgan forged cartels in selected industries, he masterminded something of an unacknowledged cartel among Wall Street banks. In *The House of Morgan*, I coined the term "Gentleman Banker's Code" to describe the unwritten rules that governed relations between premier banks and their borrowers, a code that had originated in the City of London. Under its terms, companies agreed to exclusive, comprehensive relations with their banker; if it was learned that they had even talked to competitors, they would be politely shown the door. Guided by this tacit agreement, banks didn't raid the employees of other firms, - didn't compete for business based on price, and certainly didn't countenance hostile takeovers. The Gentleman Banker's Code - didn't outlaw all competition, for every bank wanted to expand its client list and steal clients from competitors. We aren't talking about choirboys here. What the code guaranteed was that such competition would remain civilized and wouldn't weaken banks collectively vis-à-vis their corporate borrowers. So it turned competition into a courtly, genteel, stylized ritual, precise as a minuet. If you stole a client from another bank, you had to pretend you were doing no such thing. It had to look as if the oafish client had clumsily forced himself upon you. Most of all, you couldn't win business by foolishly cutting prices or offering better terms than other bankers. In that direction lay universal peril.

In early 1912, a year before J. P. Morgan's death, the firm tore down its ornate old building, with the catercorner entrance, at Broad and Wall. In 1914, it unveiled a much smaller, more elegant structure that still broods over the corner today. (Alas, it is a ghostly sort of brooding, for J.P. Morgan & Company fled down the street to a glistening skyscraper at 60 Wall Street in the 1980s.) This new building stripped away the J.P. Morgan & Co. name from above the door; hung opaque drapery over its tall, inset windows; and advertised itself to the world by the number 23 alone. Like the pearly gates of heaven, the front door would magically open to the privileged few, but was hermetically shut to less fortunate mortals.

We can now, with a little drumroll, return to my search for Rosebud, the riddle of why the old-line Wall Street and City banks shrank from anything so crass as a nameplate. The absence of a shingle reflected that the banker was a regal figure, far more important than his visitors; that his business was conducted on a don't-call-us-we'll-call-you basis; that he had no need for new clients; that it was a high honor to be received and represented by such a lofty fellow; that the bank's services were tactful and discreet; and that the banker floated high above the workaday world and felt no need to pander to public curiosity. In short, the missing nameplate signaled the private banker's temporary victory in his three-way struggle with the providers and consumers of capital. The unmarked little building was thus the ultimate in financial chic and mystique. Yet, before too long, it would testify more to past than to present glory. For even when the new 23 Wall Street opened in 1914, the public backlash was already well under way and would shatter many of the presumptions implicit in the dignified, understated architecture.

5

*T*he advent of the trusts alarmed much of America, and not just because their unholy size threatened to stifle competition in many industries and foster a lopsided distribution of power. Mirroring the influence of the Wall Street financiers and attorneys who created the trusts and piloted their fortunes, many firms shed their regional character as they were fused into huge combinations headquartered in New York. This drained economic and political power from the heartland, where the constituent companies—many of them once closely held family firms—had begun and flourished.

If confronted, J. P. Morgan would have denied that he exercised godlike control over companies and would have humbly pleaded to being one of many board members. Yet it was common knowledge on Wall Street that Morgan was invariably primus inter pares and that wherever he sat was, by definition, the chairman's seat. Never a shrinking violet on corporate boards, Morgan could register his opinions in a thunderclap voice that could shatter plate glass. If necessary, he knew how to throw a memorable, shrewdly timed temper tantrum. Growing impatient with debate that ran counter to his views, he would fling his matchbox across the room, slam his fist against the table, and bellow, "Call a vote. Let's see where these gentlemen stand." Few hardy souls, once Morgan's divine wrath was aroused, dared to cross him.

As Louis Brandeis and other reformers argued, banker-dominated boards were plainly rife with opportunities for abuse. Bankers would be tempted to encumber captive companies with too many securities and enrich themselves at their clients' expense. Indeed, after the flotation of U.S. Steel, the U.S. Bureau of Corporations said at least half of the $1.4 billion in securities represented watered stock. Yet we must note the paradox that the real clamor for liberating companies from the banker's thrall came not from the companies themselves—some of whom fairly gloried in their servitude to Morgan—but from reformers outside the financial system. One Morgan client, Charles S. Mellen, head of the New Haven Railroad, boasted to reporters, "I wear the Morgan collar, but I am proud of it. If Mr. Morgan were to order me tomorrow to China or Siberia in his interests, I would pack up and go." If Morgan was such a bloodthirsty ogre, why did his mangled victims fail to plead for their liberty? Why didn't they rattle their chains more?

One possibility is that they were too cowed and bullied to criticize their master openly. Another plausible explanation is that many board members were recruited by Morgan and therefore remained beholden to him. Yet we must also entertain a third possibility: that such bondage possessed signal advantages for companies in those days. Capital markets weren't far advanced, and investors weren't so numerous, sophisticated, or well-informed as today. A banker's seal of approval ensured that firms would enjoy unimpeded access to capital at highly attractive rates. Nowadays, we justly deplore the short-term orientation of many companies, whereas Morgan and his partners represented "patient money" and could afford to take the long view. Acting as bulwarks, they permitted young companies to ripen and develop without excessive shareholder interference. It would have been impossible in Morgan's era, with companies chained by their bankers, to have seen the terror reign of raiders, asset-strippers, and greenmailers such as stalked the Anglo-American stock exchanges in the 1980s.

In recent years, the financial press has devoted considerable space to the relative merits of the "American" banking model, characterized by an arm's-length relationship between banks and corporate clients, and the "European" model, marked by close or even exclusive banker–company relations. For the economic historian, the contrast contains richly ironic overtones, for it was Pierpont Morgan who carried the European model to its reductio ad absurdum and, in so doing, seemed to define single-handedly the future financial reform agenda in America. The European model embodied by Pierpont Morgan probably served the American economy well at this early stage in industrial development. When bankers were better known than their clients, companies stood to profit from the superior capital, cachet, and connections offered by their financial overseers. Very often it paid to take advantage of the banker's power, even if it meant sacrificing a certain amount of autonomy. As the century progressed, the entire rationale for such banker–company alliances would evaporate as the banker's middleman power waned. Yet in the late nineteenth and early twentieth centuries, the banker was strong enough, and corporations weak enough, that the European model had much to recommend it.

As a rule, Morgan and his partners chose competent managers and, despite a few notable blunders, companies prospered under their tutelage. Had they baldly fleeced companies, they - couldn't have succeeded for very long, for they would have cannibalized their own client list. That Pierpont Morgan's impact was frequently beneficial can be seen by the fact that so many of his corporate wards today number among the world's largest companies. Generations of Morgan men sat on the boards of U.S. Steel, General Motors, AT&T, and other firms either created or financed by the Morgan bank. For better or for worse, these men had a proprietary feeling toward these companies, not simply an exploitative, short-term interest. We can accuse the House of Morgan of many failings, but myopia isn't one of them.

6

*I*n our brief *tour d'horizon* of old Wall Street, we have dwelled on the dealings between bankers and corporations while slighting the role of investors. Let us hasten to make amends. In these halcyon days of banker primacy, institutional investors—insurance companies and trust companies, church and school endowments, etc.—did exist, but on an extremely modest scale by today's standards. Only after the Second World War did pension funds dramatically proliferate, spurred by collective-bargaining agreements and changes in the tax law. Even then, it took time before the stigma against investing pension-fund money in stocks waned. In 1949 it was still considered racy stuff when J.P. Morgan & Company, for the first time, bought common stocks for portfolios managed by its trust department. When General Motors permitted 50 percent of its pension-fund money to go straight into stocks—well, this seemed positively licentious to some straitlaced trust men, as if a parade of drunken Mardi Gras revelers had suddenly burst into their monastic realm. Even in the 1960s, the Ford Foundation could still stir controversy when it took its first big plunge into common stock.

And what of the status of small investors? Many of them were frankly delighted by the giant trusts that so appalled and disheartened populist critics. If these big stock issues were such barefaced swindles against the public, as all the reformers said, then these small fry were utterly thrilled to participate in them alongside titans such as Morgan. Nevertheless, most of the time, they ended up as casualties of these conspiracies, not their confederates. They seemed destined to remain the classic patsies of the investing world, the gullible latecomers whose arrival at rallies infallibly suggested that the smart money was heading for the exits. One of the savviest market operators, Bernard Baruch, famously said that when his cabbie and bootblack began to babble about stocks, he knew for certain that the market had topped out. For a long time, Wall Street had no more unerring contrary indicator than that easily bamboozled, perennial victim: the small investor.

Despite intermittent flurries of euphoria among small investors, their total number remained small and fluctuating. Typically, they would drift in and out of the market in opportunistic fashion, as the whim seized them. For the vast majority of sober citizens, however, the market seemed a shady, perilous place—a view shared, incidentally, by many a mogul. When Andrew Carnegie sold his firm to Morgan as the centerpiece of U.S. Steel, he specifically demanded payment in bonds, not trusting the watered stock. Morgan himself never darkened the Stock Exchange door, which he thought an unfit place for gentlemen, even though it loomed right across the street. Particularly in rural America, Wall Street was viewed as the haunt of dissolute city slickers. Valid reasons lay behind this anxiety. In the nineteenth century, financial panics and bank runs erupted at roughly ten-year intervals, so that everyone had fresh memories of treacherous bear markets. These wild gyrations reflected the violently cyclical nature of an economy not yet equipped with government stabilizers or a central bank that could administer that sovereign sedative in crises—liquidity. And no institutional presence tempted small investors into the market. Only in the 1920s did retail brokerage houses and securities affiliates of commercial banks tout stocks as safe bets for the middle class. The whole ethos of Wall Street remained steadfastly wholesale—that is, aloof, mysterious, and antidemocratic—a state of affairs symbolized by those nameless bank buildings.

Ordinary people were absolutely correct in thinking that the stock market was stacked against them. In fact, the capital markets were so clubby and collusive, and information so unequally distributed, that it was positively suicidal for small investors to match their wits against professionals. The market was the plaything of speculators who rigged stocks through pools and freely swapped proprietary information about companies. Not yet restrained by insider-trading laws, the market resonated like a vast whispering gallery, with only the cognoscenti of lower Manhattan in the know. Wall Street bankers didn't scruple to trade on inside information which they considered one of the finest perks of the job. (In this regard, I recall the indignation of a British friend years back who said that his broker in the City had bloody well *better* have inside information or he was moving his account elsewhere.) At bottom, the real power of old-line bankers lay in their monopoly over information, a commodity even rarer than capital in those days. Since companies didn't issue annual reports, quarterly reports, or even press releases, Wall Street bankers profited from the gross imbalance between what they knew about these companies and what the poor, benighted masses did.

Today we are accustomed to the instant dissemination of information around the globe through wire services and computer networks, placing investors on an equal footing. Early in the century, however, before such communication marvels, people in rural areas felt severely disadvantaged when it came to receiving information. Who wanted to be the last to buy on good news or sell on bad? (A fleet of carrier pigeons had sped news of major events to the Rothschilds, accounting for some of their early killings.) The stock market remained marginal to the lives of average people, who still salted away their savings in bank accounts or under the mattress. Not until 1896 did the Dow Jones Industrial Average offer a universal yardstick by which investors could judge the market's general performance. Only in 1909 did Moody's Investors Service provide its first credit ratings on railroad bonds, inaugurating an industry that would offer the public objective measures for evaluating securities. Just try to picture for a moment how blurry and all but incomprehensible investing would be without such handy aids and you will get some idea why earlier generations of investors considered the market a murky, shark-infested place.

Let us return for another glimpse at our trusty bar graph. While the banker's influence dwarfed that of corporate clients in the early 1900s, the disparity was even more profound on the investor side. In fact, the banker's hold over companies stemmed directly from the fact that investors were small and widely dispersed, offering companies no real alternative to banker control. That small investors would ever pump significant amounts of money into the stock market—that they might someday presume to mingle their savings, bypass banks, and finance companies directly through enormous mutual funds—would have seemed a preposterous flight of fancy to J. Pierpont Morgan, too absurd to warrant discussion. Had this future been clearly foreseen, the populist assault on banker power might have been mitigated, for the expansion of the stock market would more forcefully erode the banker's hegemony than the most well-meaning piece of reform legislation.

7

At this point, I would like to make a short detour into the history of the Standard Oil Company for two compelling reasons. First, the story of the oil trust previews the later liberation of large industrial concerns from the tenacious grip of their traditional bankers. The second—and no less urgent—reason is that I'm currently writing a biography of John D. Rockefeller, Sr., the founder and patron saint of Standard Oil, and can't resist dragging the poor fellow into the story.

Born in upstate New York, Rockefeller moved to Cleveland as

an adolescent, where he launched Standard Oil in 1870, eleven years after Colonel Edwin Drake drilled his famous well in western Pennsylvania. For several years, the world petroleum industry was confined to the greasy slopes of Oil Creek, a picturesque, backwoods waterway that wound between Titusville and Oil City, before spilling into the Allegheny River. Fortune hunters of every description flocked to the region, creating an overheated, boomtown atmosphere. Since nobody knew whether oil in commercial quantities existed elsewhere in the earth's crust, wildcatters tried to drain their wells as fast as possible before the whole industry vanished. Rockefeller was a deeply religious man, endowed with messianic instincts, and he was visionary enough, or maybe just plain lucky enough, to foresee a global industry arising on such unstable foundations. He possessed so many of these inspired intuitions that perhaps he did have his own private telephone line to the Lord.

After the Civil War, Wall Street bankers were so busy financing government and railroad clients that they frowned on risky industrial ventures. (We noted earlier the novelty of the Guinness share offering in London in 1886.) And the petroleum business seemed egregiously speculative to them—one reason that Rockefeller nursed a lifelong grudge against the whole banking fraternity. Even as a billionaire mogul, he made statements about bankers that sounded like the undiluted bile of some impoverished, small-town populist. A thoroughgoing Puritan, proudly self-reliant, he always made a fetish of financial self-sufficiency at Standard Oil—but only after he could afford such a luxury. As a young man, chronically short of the capital to realize his ambitions, he proved himself the champion borrower of all time. Since Wall Street lacked interest in innovation and gave entrepreneurs a frosty reception after the Civil War, most of them turned to local banks and wealthy investors for venture capital in the 1870s and 1880s. A very persuasive young Baptist, Rockefeller soon exhausted the lending capacity of Cleveland banks. In the end, the money needed to create an oil cartel forced him to look farther afield and he had to station his younger brother, William, in Manhattan to tap the resources of New York banks. John D. Rockefeller was typical of those late-nineteenth-century entrepreneurs who turned grudgingly, but inevitably, to Wall Street to carry out plans on a gigantic scale.

As it happened, Rockefeller assembled his great empire of oil refineries, pipelines, and distributors with such swift and daring efficiency that by the early 1880s Standard Oil was financially self-sufficient, and remaining so became one of the hobbyhorses of his tenure there. In his moralistic style, he sermonized upon the need to maintain large cash reserves, pay modest dividends, and finance future expansion from retained earnings. Behind this policy lurked a latent suspicion that Wall Street bankers might try to rob him of his power. As he confided to a colleague in 1885, "I think a concern so large as we are should have its own money and be independent of the 'Street.'"

By this point, Standard Oil overflowed with cash, far more than any corporation in history had produced, and far more than could be reasonably employed for its own needs. As a holding company, Standard Oil had dozens of subsidiary firms sheltered under its capacious tent. Week after week, month after month, these affiliated concerns sent their surplus revenues to 26 Broadway in lower Manhattan, seat of the Standard Oil empire. What did Standard Oil do with all this brimming cash? In the words of journalist John Moody, "in a little while, the Standard Oil Trust was really a bank of the most gigantic character—a bank within an industry, financing this industry against all competition and continually lending vast sums of money to needy borrowers on high class collateral, just as the other great banks were doing." Once again, banking arose as a natural, spontaneous offshoot of successful commerce.

These cash geysers showered down, like blessed holy water, on the National City Bank, the forerunner of today's Citicorp. It was headed by the coldly taciturn James Stillman, whose two daughters entered into dynastic marriages with the two sons of William Rockefeller. Standard Oil lavished such notable largesse upon National City that it was soon dubbed the "Standard Oil Bank." Fortified by oil money, plus his own considerable shrewdness and drive, Stillman ended up sitting on forty-one corporate boards. The critical point here is that, when people talked of National City as the "Standard Oil Bank," they meant that Standard Oil was a powerful *creditor* of the bank—that is, the trust was so big and rich that it bankrolled one of New York City's major banks. During the next generation, whenever panic roiled Wall Street, the Standard Oil treasury and John D. Rockefeller's personal fortune would inject emergency cash infusions into Wall Street banks. This foreshadowed things to come, for the twentieth century would see the growth of huge corporations that would outgrow their bankers and compete with them in banking. What makes Standard Oil so fascinating in industrial annals is that this transformation occurred a generation or two earlier than in other industries, making the trust a financial powerhouse even in the heyday of finance capitalism.

Since he was the largest individual investor in the world, the life of John D. Rockefeller, Sr., is instructive for another purpose. Through his colossal fortune and voracious appetite for high-grade securities, he often seemed less a mere earthling than an investment bank with arms and legs. In sifting through his papers and those of his chief investment adviser, a lapsed Baptist minister named Frederick T. Gates, one is struck by how restlessly Rockefeller had to prowl to locate safe securities to absorb his immense cash supply—a dilemma that seems absurdly improbable in our day of well-developed capital markets. At the time, there simply weren't enough blue-chip railroad bonds to go around, and industrial issues were still considered hazardous, as Rockefeller knew only too well from his own personal dealings with bankers. In 1911, he purchased a controlling stake in the Equitable Trust Co. precisely so that he could enter into financings with it and gain access to better securities.

In those days, rich individuals often participated as underwriters in large securities offerings, an arrangement that pointed up both the paucity of capital and the limited distribution network of investment houses, which didn't have thousands of brokers ready to stuff stocks and bonds into the accounts of pliant small investors. In many underwritings, Rockefeller took blocks of several million dollars in railroad bonds, and he was always on the qui vive for attractive new offerings from the two premier institutions, J.P. Morgan & Company, and Kuhn, Loeb, headed by the proud, unbending German-Jewish banker Jacob Schiff.

Now there may be some readers who have gnashed their teeth because their broker didn't return their calls and they felt snubbed in favor of richer clients. If so, they may be consoled by the woeful tale of poor John D. Rockefeller. He was an austere man who mistrusted pomp and show; the richer he became, the more he aspired to a monkish simplicity in his social life (at least if one sets aside the private golf courses and three-thousand-acre estate). Such a man was bound to resent the flamboyant, operatic J. P. Morgan, and their relationship reflected the age-old clash between the Roundhead and the Cavalier. When Rockefeller first met Morgan, he was repelled by what he saw as the financier's vainglory. As he recalled, "We had a few pleasant words. But I could see that Mr. Morgan was very much—well, like Mr. Morgan; very haughty, very much inclined to look down on other men. I looked at him. For my part, I have never been able to see why any man should have such a high and mighty feeling about himself." Morgan dismissed Rockefeller far more tersely: "I don't like him."

It was impossible to shake John D. Rockefeller's steely self-possession, and he was one of the few people who could truly unnerve Morgan. When Morgan created U.S. Steel, he had to deal, willy-nilly, with this nemesis, who controlled the rich iron-ore reserves on the Mesabi Range in Minnesota. In what he doubtless thought a rare mark of deference and signal departure from royal protocol, Morgan volunteered to visit Rockefeller at his office at 26 Broadway. Objecting that he was retired—true as far as it went—Rockefeller invited Morgan to call on him at his home at 4 West 54th Street, stipulating this would be a purely social occasion. For Wall Street's Jupiter to descend from the clouds and visit the home of a mortal was unprecedented. Nonetheless, the financier placed his top hat squarely on his head, set aside his pride, and went uptown. After some pleasantries, he violated Rockefeller's condition and asked him about the Mesabi ore. Rockefeller—relishing the chance to tweak his mighty guest—dryly reminded him that this was a social occasion and that he must take up the matter with his son, John D. Rockefeller, Jr., who had graduated from Brown a few years earlier. Morgan must have swallowed hard at this rebuke. When Rockefeller, Jr., then visited Morgan's office, the financier hadn't forgotten the snub and wasted no time in returning it. Conferring with a partner about legal matters, he didn't even bother to look up as the young man waited. Young Rockefeller was allowed to cool his heels for several minutes. Finally, Morgan raised his head and gave him a withering glance. In a stentorian voice, meant to blow him over, he asked, "Well, what's your price?" Rockefeller, Jr., though a shy, insecure young man, unexpectedly exhibited some of the old man's iron. "Mr. Morgan, I think there must be some mistake," he retorted. "I did not come here to sell. I understood you wished to buy." Eventually Morgan and Rockefeller concluded the deal for $88.5 million, but Morgan hadn't taken kindly to this disrespectful treatment meant to soften him up.

Because of the lively competition for inclusion in Morgan's stock-and-bond syndicates—we again stress the dearth of top-notch securities in those days—he had numerous opportunities to retaliate against investors who defied him. From Rockefeller's papers, it is clear that the offended Morgan assigned the world's richest man a lowly place in his financial hierarchy. Rockefeller became stubbornly convinced that Morgan steered him into every dud issue—especially the catastrophic North Atlantic shipping cartel, the International Mercantile Marine, and a large financing for the Chicago traction magnate Charles Yerkes—while giving him only niggardly shares of the railroad issues he prized. Understandably, Rockefeller preferred to do business with Morgan's arch-rival, Kuhn, Loeb. Today it is hard to imagine any mogul feeling neglected by his bankers, or being starved for decent securities. Rockefeller had no desire to make a big killing—he had already made the largest killing in human history—but just wanted to preserve his capital and make a decent return. At the time, that proved a very tall order. So the next time you imagine that your broker has snubbed you on some hot high-tech offering and is deliberately taunting you and kicking sand in your face, just remember the sad tale of John D. Rockefeller, Sr., who felt he could never get a fair shake from Wall Street.

8

A year after J. P. Morgan, Sr., expired at the Grand Hotel in Rome in 1913—we recall that the luckless tycoon died destitute, with only $68.3 million in his estate—the Great War broke out in Europe. Without too liberal a stretch of the historic imagination, we can credit much of Wall Street's buoyancy in the 1920s to the unforeseen consequences of that carnage. Because the U.S. government financed its war involvement through Liberty Bond drives that netted billions of dollars, it tutored millions of Americans in the virtues of securities. In this way, the government began, quite inadvertently, to wean the country away from the old bankbook style of thrift to the more glamorous but volatile regimen of stocks and bonds.

Before the 1920s, Wall Street, we have repeatedly noted, spurned the small investor as too trivial to consider. Now many of the foremost banks unveiled new securities affiliates with names that were nearly identical to their own, expressly to wipe away the old distinction between saving and speculating. Buying stocks on margin was invested with new respectability and the public rejoiced in talk of a New Era of blue skies and perpetual prosperity, as if the business cycle had been repealed forever. In this giddy environment, Wall Street discovered that it could move stocks, like soap suds or cereal, through high-pressure salesmanship. The emblematic figure was Charles Mitchell, the ex–securities salesman who rose to become head of the National City Bank and its stock subsidiary, the National City Company. Fielding a hard-charging army of 2,000 brokers, he exhorted these foot soldiers to sell, sell, sell, galvanizing them with pep talks and sales contests. Mitchell's brokers peddled stocks with all the subtlety of carnival barkers, palming off exotic, risky securities on green investors. Later on, in the aftermath of the Crash, it was disclosed that the National City Company had repackaged bum Latin American loans from its affiliated bank and fobbed them off on feckless investors—one of the outrages that sparked the retributive Glass-Steagall Act, which separated commercial from investment banking. We should note that at least one banking scholar, George J. Benston of Emory University, has argued that such improprieties never took place.

Those readers who have been pestered by unwanted phone calls from brokers with loud, grating voices will be interested to learn that the "cold call" was born in the 1920s. The writer Matthew Josephson, hired as a young Jazz Age broker, told a splendid story that evoked the predatory atmosphere of the time.

As he and his colleagues dialed their way down cold-calling lists, he eavesdropped on a neighbor, who telephoned one number and was told that the party he was trying to reach was dead. Without missing a beat, the young broker asked, "Well, can I please speak to the next of kin?" The decade spawned new financial products as well, including the unit trust, better known in our day as the mutual fund. We like to think that the major rationale for mutual funds is that they provide safety and diversification, but in the 1920s they were soon perverted into speculative vehicles. Many of these highly leveraged investment trusts invested in other highly leveraged investment trusts, throwing up precarious new pyramids of debt that all came tumbling down in October 1929.

Because the Roaring Twenties are so identified with the effervescent stock market, one is startled to learn how few people actually played the market. The estimates range from 1 million to 3 million people. For the great majority of Americans, the 1929 Crash probably occasioned little mourning and one suspects that, in many small towns and farms, the news was greeted with grim satisfaction, as if messengers told of the destruction of Sodom and Gomorrah. Yes, people doubtless said with a sigh, what a pity that such multitudes should perish, but hadn't they brought it upon themselves with their wicked ways? Few suspected that the Crash was the curtain-raiser for an enduring depression that would afflict every household, including those that had savored the *Schadenfreude* of October 1929. As for the chastened small investors, scorched by the fire and brimstone, they swore that they would never again be hoodwinked and deserted the stock market for a generation, some forever.

Bankers are used to being called many nasty names and tend to develop thick rinds, but even this hardy breed was taken aback when they were called "banksters"—rhyming with "gangsters"—during the New Deal era. How did one explain that to the wife and children at the dinner table? On the surface, the 1930s seemed a moribund period for financial markets, a long breather after all the frenzied speculation. Yet the lethal calm was somewhat deceptive, for a critical, self-correcting mechanism was already at work. By ending the easy margin requirements of the 1920s, New Deal regulators blotted a lot of the speculative froth from future bull markets. Of all the legislation enacted, it was the Securities Act of 1933, with its strong disclosure requirements, that would make the postwar world safe for shareholder democracy. Those who framed the laws cleverly deprived bankers of their historic monopoly on information. By forcing companies to file registration statements and make information publicly available on a nondiscriminatory basis, they equalized the status of company insiders and small investors on the outside. The shadowy world of banker–client relations was suddenly and brilliantly disinfected with sunlight. Just how revolutionary the development was would not be apparent for fifty years. At this point, let us simply note that bankers could no longer trade securities based on superior information about companies, nor could they shield corporate clients from the harsh scrutiny of the stock market.

Because some banks had secretly converted their grubby bad loans into shiny new securities, the New Deal reformers passed the Glass-Steagall Act, which ended the system of universal banking that had prevailed until that time. Henceforth, the industry would be divided into commercial banks, which took deposits and made loans, and investment banks, which originated, traded, and distributed securities. Most small-town banks on the dusty Main Streets of America had never dabbled in the securities business to begin with and were unaffected by Glass-Steagall; to this day they staunchly defend the act, however, hoping to deprive their big-city brethren from adding fresh weapons to their arsenals and thus putting them at a competitive disadvantage.

For the House of Morgan and other mandarin firms situated in the maze of lower Manhattan, the act had a shattering impact.

It was bad enough that they had to retrench and lose profitable business during the Depression, but the act dealt an even greater blow by eroding the traditional banker system. Only a universal bank could offer an all-inclusive range of services and demand that a client deal with it exclusively. If a company now had to raise loans from one bank and market securities with another, it would need, at a minimum, two bankers—opening the door to that most dreadful thing, competition. Admittedly, the banker could insist upon a modified version of the Gentleman Banker's Code—that is, that the investment bank would handle all securities offerings for a given client—and that indeed happened in subsequent decades. At the same time, it destroyed forever the possibility that a J. Pierpont Morgan—Omnipotent Ruler of the Universe, advising companies on all their financial needs—could ever emerge again.

Such was the power of Glass-Steagall that, whereas J. Pierpont Morgan had been a name to conjure with in his day, Wall Street executives of the 1950s would be a colorless breed, unknown to the general public, like so many gray-haired bureaucrats. One can justly argue that the House of Morgan badly bungled things in the 1930s by opting to become a commercial bank and spinning off a securities house, Morgan Stanley. The bank didn't anticipate that corporate clients would someday find it cheaper to raise money in the capital markets than from bank credit. In hindsight, it seems a shocking failure of vision for a firm that had sponsored $6 billion in securities for blue-chip companies and foreign governments between the end of the First World War and F.D.R.'s inauguration. After the passage of Glass-Steagall, a Morgan partner, Russell Leffingwell, wrote a letter to President Roosevelt, urging repeal of the act in the following terms: "The business of underwriting capital issues is and should be a by-product business. It is occasional and sporadic. Nobody can afford to be in the business unless he has a good bread and butter business to live on. A house exclusively in the underwriting business is under too much pressure to pay overhead and living expenses to pick and choose the issues it will underwrite."

Leffingwell was an erudite man, the resident philosopher-king, yet his reasoning here seems monumentally shortsighted. In the future, the investment-banking business would be anything but "occasional" or "sporadic." Nonetheless, mired in the deep, terminal gloom of the mid-1930s, even the most farsighted Morgan partners had no idea how vast and vibrant capital markets would be by the year 2000. Surely their vision was dimmed by the hopeless world outside their window, the persisting economic stagnation. The international capital markets were all but shut down while, at the New York Stock Exchange, bored traders played games to kill off the ennui. In those drab times, it must have been hard to picture a new generation of fresh-faced young investors, avidly scanning the stock-market page and flocking to their neighborhood brokers. At such a time, it would have taken exceptional foresight, perhaps superhuman clairvoyance, to visualize a world in which tens of millions of ardent investors—and not traditional bankers—would someday determine the fate of mighty corporations. For the moment, Wall Street seemed to lie in a deep coma from which it would never awaken.

9

At the end of the Second World War, scarred by hard times, investors grimly anticipated the resumption of the Depression. Instead, buoyed by the huge, stimulative jolt of the Second World War—the ultimate experiment in pump priming—the American economy and stock market rebounded from the prolonged malaise of the 1930s. In 1954 the Dow Jones Industrial Average finally managed to regain the heights achieved on the eve of the 1929 Crash. With the hostile powers, Germany and Japan, still prostrate from the war, American multinational corporations enjoyed that surreal, evanescent honeymoon when they seemed to lack any stiff competition in global markets. During this interregnum, they accumulated the capital and connections, the high-flying credit ratings and financial acumen, that should have freed them from the grip of bankers forever.

Oddly enough, it didn't happen. The wonder was that the old captivity continued, albeit in a new attenuated form mandated by Glass-Steagall. The slaves hugged their chains, as if they were a security blanket. Consider the high-handed policies that Morgan Stanley dared to impose on its submissive clients throughout the 1950s and 1960s. Like Pierpont Morgan back in the Teddy Roosevelt era, the firm demanded exclusive relations for security offerings and perpetuated several ancient rituals. The firm had to be the sole manager of underwritings, so that it could choose other syndicate members and pocket the full fee for "running the books." Morgan Stanley made other outrageous demands. In the tall, rectangular "tombstone ads" that list syndicate members in the morning papers, Morgan Stanley had to appear alone, in solitary glory, in the upper left-hand corner. Printers of the ads had to employ a special typeface called "Ronaldson Slope." Finally, all Morgan prospectuses were to be printed in royal blue, a fitting shade indeed, for royal courts had once enforced such absurd rituals to trumpet their absolute power. From the perspective of a later day, it all seems slightly mad, yet a blue-ribbon roster of corporate names—including General Motors, U.S. Steel, General Electric, AT&T, and IBM—submitted to these arbitrary rules.

At a time before companies employed derivatives and other complex hedging strategies, investment banks had little incentive to innovate and offered a staple list of services to docile clients. (If a company issued a security with some ingenious new wrinkle, investors assumed the company must be in trouble, or why had it bothered to deviate from the norm?) No self-respecting banker hustled for clients (at least not too openly) and new clients still seemed to show up, unbidden, on the doorstep. A high IQ was less important for Wall Street employment than a well-tailored suit, an agreeable manner, and an extensive network of old school ties. In this sedate world, a partner could still place a misfit son or ne'er-do-well nephew on the payroll without doing irreparable harm to the firm. The main thing was to preserve relationships, which meant being pleasant, courteous, and efficient. Because they stuck to their traditional role as middlemen, investment banks had the luxury of small staffs and modest capital. In 1962, Morgan Stanley had $7 million in capital and 110 employees, versus $12 billion in capital and 10,000 employees by 1995. As private partnerships, they didn't need to attend to the interests of shareholders who might have been upset by the vagaries of the securities markets and the resulting fluctuations in profits.

Unbeknownst to these privileged, preppy financiers as they gaily lunched and golfed their way through the week, the twilight of the old Wall Street was gathering. If investment banking retained many of the trappings and perquisites of power, the basis of that power had long since fled. In the early 1900s, a Pierpont Morgan could afford to take a supercilious attitude toward fledgling firms such as General Motors and American Telephone & Telegraph. Now these same clients were big, strong, multinational corporations, infinitely better known than their Wall Street bankers and often with better credit ratings. Many could have flouted Morgan Stanley's rules, but they refused to do so. When I mentioned this puzzling behavior to grizzled Morgan veterans of that era, they tended to shrug their shoulders, still mystified that their clients allowed themselves to be so easily cowed. Why - didn't the old system crumble sooner? Why were the participants, in retrospect, so blind to the power shift?

The only way I can explain this bizarre phenomenon is to recall a visit I made as a novice journalist to a Pennsylvania bull stud. The star tenants were two- and three-ton bulls—bovine tanks of truly terrifying power—who were meekly led about by rings in their noses. When I first arrived at the stud early one morning, I watched a slim man named Floyd, clad in a spotless apron, meticulously collect semen from the bulls as they reared up and mounted eunuch bulls before thunderously clattering back to earth. Afterward, as we amiably chatted, Floyd led me down a long barn lined with cinderblock stalls that housed the bulls. He imparted a fascinating tidbit of information: these beasts were so powerful that they could have kicked their way out of the stalls to freedom in the lovely meadow outside; they simply - didn't know their own strength. In dealing with Wall Street investment banks in the 1950s and 1960s, blue-chip corporations resembled those dim-witted bulls. They were paralyzed by vestigial fears, those half-remembered admonitions, probably first heard as young executives, about not antagonizing their Wall Street banker. They were afraid to test their power, lest they be struck dead by lightning bolts.

If the bankers at Morgan Stanley, Kuhn, Loeb, and other blue-blooded houses had studied my tripartite bar graph in the 1960s, they would have noticed two startling—and, from their viewpoint, extremely ominous—developments during the previous generation. On the one hand, the capital consumers—the *Fortune* 500 companies—had grown indescribably huge during the Pax Americana and no longer needed a bank's imprimatur. This was less astounding than what had happened to the capital providers through the stupendous growth of institutional investors from corporate pension funds to mutual funds. A multitude of trends—to be examined in due course—were forcing people to set aside more money for their retirement years. Companies were setting up defined benefit plans that bolstered the power of institutional money managers at the expense of small investors. The power of the wholesale banker was shrinking—maybe not in absolute terms, but surely in relation to the dramatic growth of both their clients and customers. For the first time in the twentieth century, the middleman was dwarfed by the other two pillars of the financial community.

While the fancy Wall Street houses kept their attention firmly fixed on their corporate clients, a group of clever, scrappy firms, with a much better strategic sense, turned their attention in the other direction. Morgan Stanley and similar "bulge bracket" firms had long retained a snobbish distaste for trading securities, considering it undignified for white-shoe bankers. (Remember the sociology of relationship banking: it needed people from good schools and clubs, and such people preferred easy sedentary jobs and long lunch hours. Who can blame them?) Stepping into this breach, Salomon Brothers and Goldman, Sachs began to exploit their trading desks to win over the new institutional investors, pension plans and bank trust departments, who had complex needs as they traded huge, unwieldy blocks of stock. By courting institutional investors, these assertive, upstart houses—long derided as part of the Wall Street peasantry—began to chip away at the dominance of Morgan Stanley, Kuhn, Loeb et al. To its credit, Morgan Stanley woke up fast, began building a trading operation and distribution network, and became a fully integrated investment bank—albeit one lacking a retail distribution network. Kuhn, Loeb and other drowsy rivals who dozed off in the 1950s were slow to adapt and never awoke from their slumber.

The days of the traditional banker were numbered, and it required only a good test case to prove it. The inevitable showdown came in 1979, when IBM rang down the curtain on the long-running drama of wholesale bankers and their captive clients. Although Morgan Stanley had been its traditional investment banker, IBM decided to flout Morgan's rules and bring in that aggressive arriviste, Salomon Brothers, to co-manage a billion-dollar debt issue. After an emotional meeting, the Morgan Stanley directors decided they could not tolerate such a scandalous precedent, lest it embolden their other shackled clients. So they refused to co-operate with IBM on a billion-dollar issue, believing the company would back down. This was a serious misreading of history. Big Blue blithely sent back word that Salomon Brothers would head the new issue—without Morgan Stanley. The magic spell was bro-ken, the slaves were freed from the plantation, and other firms rushed in to raid Morgan Stanley's client list. Before long—just as Morgan Stanley had feared—everybody was poaching everybody else's clients as the genteel competition dictated by the Gentleman Banker's Code all but disappeared. The spirited competition that replaced it had been the goal sought by reformers since Pierpont Morgan's day. Now it came about, not by legislative fiat or regu-latory decree, but thanks to the spontaneous operation of mar-ket forces. The stage had been conveniently set for the stock market–dominated Wall Street of the 1980s and 1990s.

As the world of relationship banking faded, it was replaced by the fast, anonymous, much less comfortable world of transac-tional banking. (The London financial press drew a nice distinc-tion between the old-fashioned "gentlemen" and the emerging "players,"showing the same forces at work among the City's mer-chant banks.) Free of the old monogamous relationships, corpo-rate clients promiscuously flirted with many financial-service firms. They turned to different bankers for different services and played one off against another to negotiate the best possible terms. With all major companies now operating in a global arena, they also entertained foreign bankers and developed separate net-works of overseas advisers. No longer was it unusual for a blue-chip company to enlist ten different bankers in the space of a year. Still more troubling for the bankers, more and more companies placed their debt directly with institutional investors, eliminating the banker's role altogether. The strength of the middleman was rapidly declining, while the power of the providers and consumers of capital continued to grow exponentially, tightening the squeeze on Wall Street.

As long as underwriting was a profitable business, the old-line Wall Street partnerships required little capital and could remain sedate, discreet, and intimate, much like Ivy League alumni clubs. With the new dominance of trading and distribution, investment banking suddenly required enormous amounts of capital, which would finally force many of these firms to go public in the 1970s and 1980s. And that, in turn, would mean that the same wholesale bankers who had once cracked the whip over the country's largest companies would now themselves be subject to the control of money managers and other outsiders. And these investors, in time, would be mightily dissatisfied with the product mix and revenue streams of the great investment banking houses, forcing them into revolutionary adaptations.

1 0

*B*efore moving on to our thrilling finale—the brave new world of Wall Street in the 1980s and 1990s, and the irrevocable rout of bankers by shareholders as the masters of corporate destiny— I would like to digress and consider two anachronistic cases in which bank-based economies have survived: Germany and Japan. These two countries may be thought of as the Jurassic Parks of the financial world, where dinosaurs who have perished elsewhere still lumber ponderously through the jungle, munching on vegetation and wreaking havoc. Both countries are now experiencing belated reactions against banker domination and are reenacting dramas that have long since faded from memory in the United States. It may be an auspicious moment to ask why bankers in those countries have kept their preeminent place and why they are now in such serious straits.

To fathom the logic of any financial system, one must range beyond the narrow bounds of finance. Banking systems don't hover off in the ether somewhere, detached from society, but are deeply embedded in larger political and economic structures. As we have seen, the so-called American model of transparent financial markets and shareholder democracy didn't just arise spontaneously in the marketplace but rather represented, at least in part, a political reaction to market forces. Any country with America's deep antipathy to centralized political power wasn't likely to tolerate for very long the excessive power bottled up in banker-company alliances. As I argued earlier, the early stages of industrial development naturally generate such alliances because of the temporary weaknesses of infant industries and the comparative strength of the bankers who nourish them with capital. The mystery is perhaps less why such alliances appear—for they seem to answer to an eternal economic logic—than why they persist in some countries.

I would first emphasize that both Germany and Japan, early in this century, had political cultures that were deeply conservative, with some frightening, authoritarian tendencies. When political elites scorn and manipulate the masses, corporate elites will likely exhibit parallel contempt for shareholders; in despotic societies, power tends to be concentrated at the top in both political and economic institutions. Take away political democracy, and shareholder democracy is far less likely to flourish. As a rule, democratic societies will curb unbridled power exercised jointly by bankers and corporations. By the same token, democratic societies will find shareholder democracy—where corporate managers are held accountable and can be "voted from office" by disgruntled shareholders—highly congenial and compatible with the general rules of the political game.

It is ironic that the United States was moving to tame banker power just as the opposite tendency was at work in Germany. As we have seen, Pierpont Morgan reorganized the railroads and orchestrated the great wave of trusts with awesome thoroughness in the 1890s and early 1900s. In consequence, by the time of Woodrow Wilson's reform administration in the 1910s, the United States was strengthening its antitrust legislation. In 1927, Congress further throttled banker power by enacting the McFadden Act, which prohibited interstate expansion by banks. Behind these policies lay an American ideal—often, admittedly, honored more in the breach than in the observance—that vigorous competition among small-scale economic units would lead to optimal results in industry and finance. In the end, American industrial corporations would find it far easier to circumvent political checks on their power than would the banks, which were heavily regulated and subject to political oversight.

Such ideals had never taken root in Germany, which honored economic and political concentration. Even before the First World War, the large deposit banks had gone through several waves of mergers and consolidations, producing eight major banks. The German government made no effort to obstruct the growth of giant banks, nor did it feel obliged to fragment the financial system for political ends, and the banks expanded in tandem with German industry. In the mid-1920s, they helped to consummate a series of gigantic consolidations that produced new trusts in many industries. Daimler joined Benz, the United Steel Works (second only to Morgan's U.S. Steel) emerged, and six large chemical companies collaborated to form that great German behemoth, I.G. Farben. These combinations were largely effected under the aegis of bankers who could attract the foreign capital that made them possible. In exchange, they took stakes in these companies, became their principal bankers, and reserved the right to lead their future lending consortia. When the 1931 banking crisis came, these shareholdings plunged in value, gravely weakening the banks' balance sheets.

A strong bank tends to consolidate its grip on client companies during periods of economic crisis—one thinks of Morgan bat-
tening on the bankrupt railroads in the 1890s. Since German
history was riddled with crises, the everlasting turmoil presented
innumerable opportunities for bankers to strengthen their hold.
The string of seemingly unending economic disasters that over-
took Germany—including the confiscation of property abroad
during the First World War, the 1923 hyperinflation, and the financial collapse of the early 1930s—forced many ailing companies into extreme dependency upon bankers, who saved them by
swapping debt for equity. Businessmen who have endured economic dislocation prefer a banker's steady presence to the potentially fickle support of shareholders. Even today, many corporate
holdings in German bank portfolios date from prewar salvage
operations. Such a troubled history was almost guaranteed to
produce close ties between domineering banks and vulnerable
corporate clients.

Unlike Wall Street in the 1910s or 1930s, the German banks
never faced a day of reckoning at the hands of irate reformers.
There was simply too much political turmoil for economic reform
to stand high on the agenda. The popular hostility that might
have been turned against banks was projected outward against
the authors of the Versailles Treaty or against Jewish financiers in
the 1930s. So while Washington grilled bankers before Congressional committees and dismembered universal banks in the 1930s,
the Nazis betrayed no comparable zeal for financial reform. In
preparing for war, they actually welcomed banker control over
companies—the three largest banks were effectively nationalized
for five years after the 1931 banking crisis—which made it much
easier to exert bureaucratic guidance over a war-oriented economy.

Unless the aim was to despoil Jews of their businesses, the
Nazis had no more desire to disperse power in the banking than
in the political sphere. They offered Jewish bankers, such as M.M.

Warburg & Company in Hamburg, three options: they could liquidate their banks, sell out to larger non-Jewish banks, or "Aryanize" their banks—that is, hand over control to non-Jews. This last option was chosen by the Warburgs, who hoped someday to return to Germany. But many Jewish bankers entertained no such hopes, selling out at distress-sale prices to large deposit banks, and this purge of Jewish bankers consolidated the banking system even further.

After years of dictatorship and economic dislocation, Germany wearily emerged from the Second World War with an exaggerated need for stability. In this national quest for industrial harmony, many companies granted unions seats on corporate boards under the system of codetermination. They sought to cushion workers from marketplace rigors, and this included the sometimes unsparing judgments of a system based on stock-market control. Stability had a far higher priority than innovation. Neither managers, workers, nor bankers wanted to appease meddlesome shareholders who might demand layoffs, restructurings, or laborsaving measures to enhance profitability. In many ways, banks were the linchpins of the system. They held commanding blocks of stock, voted proxy shares, provided loans, and sat on supervisory boards of companies, often supplying the chairmen. Armed with such powers, they protected companies from corporate raiders, money managers, or other interlopers who might tear apart the whole delicate web of labor–management relations. For several decades, this system worked extremely well, producing prosperity and stability; only now do we see that these benefits often came at the price of long-term stagnation. Perhaps the real German economic miracle was that a system tailor-made to produce expensive labor, ossified management, and complacent banks succeeded as well as it did for so long.

Under the tutelage of their "house banks," many German companies didn't bother to sell shares to the public. Instead, the structure of the system dictated that banks load up client companies with old-fashioned bank loans. Of course, corporate treasurers knew they were relying on an increasingly antiquated form of financing and could save money by issuing commercial paper and securities. Yet they willingly sacrificed such ready savings because they valued their bank connections and didn't wish to disclose information to snooping strangers. (German business is notoriously, obsessively, secretive.) Somewhere in the psyche of pessimistic German businessmen, the banker was still revered as a strongman who would steer the company through hard times. And in German history, God knows, there had been hard times galore.

This obsolete system is now unraveling for several reasons. The German government has begun to bemoan the absence of an *Aktienkultur,* or shareholding culture, that would expedite the privatization of Deutsche Telekom, the post office bank, and state-owned real estate. Humbled by their own turbulent history, German investors are risk-averse and have been content to plough their retirement savings into low-interest bank certificates, bonds, and old-fashioned insurance policies. The government of Chancellor Helmut Kohl would like to scale back Germany's expensive system of retirement benefits by replacing it with an American-style system of private pension funds and mutual funds. To the extent that the German government succeeds in diverting household savings from safe, low-risk securities into the stock market, they will provide German companies with an alternative to dependence on bankers.

Perhaps the major impetus for change will come from the companies themselves. Many small German companies are eager to go public and would welcome the legions of adventurous stock-market investors such as exist in America, where new, obscure companies can find a friendly reception that would be unimaginable in Europe. In the medium-sized, family-owned firms which make up the so-called German *Mittelstand*, many founders are dying off or planning for their successors. Often the only feasible way to find the capital to perpetuate and renovate their aging firms is to convert them to publicly traded companies. As for Germany's industrial giants, they yearn to cash in on the pension and mutual-fund boom in the Anglo-Saxon world and secure listings on foreign stock exchanges. (For tax reasons, German companies finance pensions with reserves on their books instead of with pension funds.) Needing cheap capital to expand, these companies feel trapped in the anemic, lackluster German capital markets and enviously eye their counterparts abroad.

As universal banks, the German banks should have been flexible and versatile enough to switch from bank loans to underwritings and shepherd their clients into global markets. But after so many plodding, unimaginative decades of force-feeding clients bank loans, the stodgy German banks have proved sadly deficient in providing such services to their clients. While Deutsche Bank and other large banks have tried to expand their global capacity to trade and distribute securities—often buying into overseas investment banking by wooing star bankers with bountiful compensation packages—the American investment banks have unashamedly wooed traditional German companies eager to sample the illicit pleasures of the international capital markets.

As more German companies defect from traditional bankers and tap global capital markets, they will have to adapt to the tougher accounting standards and disclosure laws prevalent in the Anglo-Saxon world. Prohibited from engaging in stock buybacks and other methods of enhancing shareholder value, large German companies have, until recently, been oblivious to their performance on the stock exchange. Executives wouldn't deign to chat with mutual-fund managers, nor would individual investors receive an especially hospitable reception if they called for information. It was the same attitude that had typified American industry in the late nineteenth and early twentieth centuries, and for much the same reason: shares weren't widely enough distributed to warrant any particular regard for public opinion. Now, with nascent activism among their shareholders, German companies can no longer be so arrogantly reclusive. As they turn abroad for capital to survive, many of them have, for the first time, significant foreign share-ownership. Nearly half the shares of three major pharmaceutical companies, for instance—Hoechst, Bayer, and Schering—are now foreign-owned. As a result, one hears German managers starting to spout the lingo of "shareholder value" and "corporate governance"—concepts so new and alien to most Germans that the language has no real terms to express them.

In this context, Daimler-Benz's situation is revealing. As Germany's largest industrial conglomerate, it sells everything from airplanes to autos. For a long time, with nearly one-quarter of its shares owned by Deutsche Bank, the concern felt no need to curry favor with small shareholders. When Juergen Schrempp became Daimler-Benz chairman in 1995, he telephoned twenty senior managers with the identical question: what did they think of the company's share price? The question was hardly a brainteaser, yet only two of the twenty had the faintest notion of the quotation. Schrempp's action was prompted by Daimler's New York Stock Exchange listing, which has subjected the company to stricter accounting and fuller disclosure policies than those in Germany. The cryptic, hermetic world of Daimler-Benz was suddenly thrown up to the glare of public appraisal. Once the company's performance became a matter of public record, it had to meet the same performance standard demanded of any other stock and provide the same information. It no longer had the option of being a poor, sluggish performer, cosseted by its banker and indifferent to shareholders.

German dissatisfaction with the old bank-based system has

lately centered upon Deutsche Bank, with its more than $500 billion in assets. Many of the charges being leveled against the bank have eerie echoes of fin de siècle Wall Street, when Pierpont Morgan, as director of and banker to many firms, was chastised for presiding over too many client companies. It has also been accused of exercising poor supervision with several troubled borrowers. At this point, Deutsche Bank would welcome the chance to lighten its $15-billion stock portfolio, invested in more than a dozen companies, so as to free up capital for other, more profitable, purposes. The main thing restraining the bank is a punitive capital-gains tax of 60 percent. Since it took stock in many companies decades ago, the market value for these shares now far exceeds their book value and would produce an exorbitant tax bill if the stocks were sold. If the capital-gains tax is lowered in Germany and banks begin to unwind their industrial holdings, the effect will be revolutionary. The move from a bank-based to a market-based system would expose German business, for the first time, to the relentless judgment of the stock market. Yes, it would open up the economy to all the modern evils of Wall Street, from marauding corporate raiders to junk bonds to debt-heavy leveraged buyouts, but it would also release a lot of pent-up competitive energy, galvanize sleepy companies, and shake up the staid hierarchical structure of German society. On balance, I think, it would be for the best.

For a time in the 1980s, the elephantine size of the Japanese banks—some of them bulging with hundreds of billions of dollars in assets—petrified the financial world. Aided by the strong yen, they gobbled up prestige properties across America, absorbed much of the U.S. budget deficit, and opened branch networks around the globe. They seemed so big and muscular, so swollen with capital, that it was hard to conceive how the Lilliputian

Americans or Europeans could possibly rival these Brobdingna-gians of global banking. Even today, seven of the ten largest banks in the world, as measured by assets, are Japanese.

In retrospect, we can see that their hypertrophied girth was symptomatic of weakness, not strength, that these muscle-bound banks were closer to Richard Nixon's celebrated image of a "piti-ful, helpless giant" than to the samurai bankers of myth. For sev-eral years now, the large Japanese banks have reeled from a debt crisis so grave that some observers claim that their solvency is a polite fiction, perpetuated by a government afraid of touching off financial panic. The banking authorities have admitted to hun-dreds of billions of dollars in bad loans, but independent analysts dismiss even such stupefying numbers as figures of art, and peg the real damage at closer to $1 trillion. Japan's worst lending cri-sis since the Second World War has exposed many weaknesses camouflaged by the "bubble economy" of the 1980s. As we shall see, what ails the Japanese banks is the same malady that has af-flicted the big German banks—they are strapped to a dying lend-ing business.

Since the late nineteenth century, the Japanese banks have operated as engines of growth, powering the massive industrial groups, or zaibatsu—Mitsubishi, Sumitomo, Mitsui, and so on—that sprang up along with the European and American trusts of the day. Each zaibatsu was controlled by a different family, with a banking house as its hub; almost all of these banks, with the out-standing exception of Mitsui, restricted their operations to the family group. In a manner reminiscent of Germany, the foremost banks profited from a series of crises in the interwar period that weeded out weak banks and entrenched the strong. The 1923 earthquake, which left more than 100,000 dead in Japan, initiated a lending boom as the country struggled to recover. Through a complex sequence of events, this led to a deflation and dozens of bank failures by 1927. After a two-day bank "holiday"—a lovely euphemism that seems to be popular among politicians everywhere—and a three-week moratorium on unrestricted deposit withdrawals, the government enacted legislation to consolidate the banking system. Since the five major zaibatsu banks had sailed through these rough seas unharmed, they grew enormously as a result of the panic. In a striking parallel to Germany, the government solidified already close ties between Japanese banks and industry during the war. In 1943, it teamed up munitions companies with "authorized financial institutions" and thereby set the stage for the symbiotic banker–client ties of the postwar era.

During the postwar American occupation of Japan, some lingering New Deal fervor spilled over into Japan when General Douglas MacArthur introduced a Japanese version of Glass-Steagall, Article 65, to separate banking and securities work. Because the zaibatsu were almost trademarks of Japanese militarism, the American occupation authorities moved to disband them. Such reforms proved cosmetic and fleeting. Instead of disappearing, the zaibatsu evolved, in a subtle, indirect Japanese fashion, into the keiretsu, or "affiliations," that governed the postwar economy. Through extensive cross-shareholdings with client firms, Japanese banks resurrected the leadership role played by zaibatsu holding companies before the war. Like their German counterparts, Japanese banks heaped cheap loans upon client companies until they staggered under unhealthy debt burdens. Where American companies would soon abandon banks for the stock-and-bond market, the chained Japanese companies had no such tempting escapes. As partial owners of these companies, Japanese banks reined in wayward clients while Article 65 excluded banks and their corporate clients from the tightly restricted securities markets. The absence of an active commercial paper market threw up another roadblock to outside financing. Adding to this rigor mortis, the ministry of finance restricted long-term financing to a group of long-term credit banks. Even Japan's tax and regulatory structure conspired to tether companies to their banks. Granted their virtual monopoly on blue-chip lending, bankers basked in such a privileged position in the early postwar years that Japan, in global financial circles, earned the sobriquet of the "Bankers' Kingdom." Heaven was about to degenerate into hell.

As a vanquished nation, postwar Japan—like Germany—favored growth, security, and stability over such expendable frills as corporate profitability and a high return on assets. Banks functioned as huge mills that churned deposits into cheap loans for corporations. For a long time, this system hummed along nicely and everything seemed harmonious in the well-oiled banking world. Since the government fixed lending rates, companies had no incentive to shop for better terms and enrage their traditional bankers. In this hidebound, rule-bound world, bankers behaved more like diligent civil servants than enterprising businessmen and failed to pioneer in sophisticated new services, such as derivatives, or advanced back-office technologies. Wholesale lending was accepted as a loss leader for banks. Right through the 1990s, they set paper-thin margins on corporate loans that were infinitesimally higher than their funding costs—sometimes by a quarter, even an eighth, of a percentage point. When you factor in the cost of administering these loans and setting aside capital for possible default, the banks probably lost money on many big loans. Where Citibank currently earns a 6.7 percent return on loans and investments, Fuji Bank makes a preposterously low 1.3 percent on average. The Japanese banks can scarcely afford this systematic giveaway, for large corporate loans have accounted for about 30 percent of the business of Japan's big commercial or "city" banks.

After this prolonged, mostly happy, if terminally boring, marriage, Japanese banks and large corporations have approached a point of separation, even divorce. As always happens with broken marriages, the romance had quietly begun to cool long before the matrimonial lawyers arrived. In the late 1970s, Japanese companies turned to floating Eurodollar bonds for money, reducing their dependency upon their traditional "city" banker at home. By the 1980s, Japanese companies, flush with cash from their spectacular export boom, drifted even farther away from reliance on bankers. They wallowed in so much money that they gambled in the stock market with the surplus—a practice known as zaitech—and even aped their bankers, lending money to subsidiary firms. Then interest rates were deregulated in the 1990s and companies lost their incentive to stay hitched to their historic bankers. In the newly competitive environment, it became self-destructive not to scout around for the best deal. Where companies in the early postwar years felt blissfully coddled by their bankers, who ensured them access to scarce capital, they now felt imprisoned in an antediluvian system that had lost its original rationale.

The relationship has frayed at both ends. In the heady stock market of the 1980s, the shareholdings of Japanese banks appreciated enormously and fattened their capital. They looked as plump, rosy, and happy as sumo wrestlers. When the bubble economy was punctured, however, the value of their stock holdings contracted and perilously shrank their capital, threatening to drag them below the stiff new global capital requirements set by the Bank for International Settlements. The whole boom had been premised on strength in real estate prices; when those prices plunged, they wiped out the collateral behind many loans. As bad debts piled up to an alarming extent, the banks had to augment cash reserves against bad loans, forcing them to start liquidating their huge portfolios of securities—the same securities that had kept their keiretsu clients bound and gagged for so long. From the banks' standpoint, this unwinding of their stakes hasn't been a total disaster. If the truth be told—and it is never spoken too loudly—it has probably gratified some secret, long-postponed wishes. Many banks had begun to chafe at the low returns they reaped on their portfolios and yearned to redeploy this capital to better effect; they were tired of propping up overextended clients at nominal interest rates. The banking crisis thus provided a convenient cover to act on unspoken desires. As in Europe and America, the rationale behind relationship banking has all but perished in Japan and the bankers have discovered, under duress, that they can no longer operate as philanthropic institutions.

Faced with the demise of standard lending to large companies, the Japanese banks, like their peers in other countries, now court small and medium-sized borrowers and individuals that lack access to capital markets. They have been agitating for freedom from the regulatory straitjacket that has barred them from selling life insurance and mutual funds. The Japanese authorities recognize that Article 65 is passé, lashing Japanese banks and businesses to an obsolete lending business. Almost all Japanese banks now boast securities subsidiaries that can service large corporate customers through the capital markets, much as they have done in the Eurobond market for years. Bowing to the inevitable, the government of Ryutaro Hashimoto has recently announced, amid great fanfare, a "Big Bang" for Tokyo's financial markets by the year 2001 that will tear down the remaining boundaries among banking, brokerage, and life insurance and permit universal banks.

In Japan, one can broadly discern the outlines of a transition from a system that revolved around powerful banks to one based on the stock market. Of the trends now under way, perhaps the most significant is the slow-motion dissolution of the cross-shareholding system. A survey published two years ago suggested that industrial companies and banks hoarded as much as three-quarters of all Japanese stock to establish their economic groupings. As these shares are sold in the open market and divided among myriad shareholders, the prices of Japanese stocks will genuinely reflect corporate performance rather than the protection of banking patrons or corporate alliances. In time, Japanese corporations will develop greater sensitivity to shareholder concerns and may even have to contend with the potential menace of hostile takeovers. No longer swaddled inside the cocoons of banks and insurance companies, they will be exposed to the bracing vicissitudes of the stock market. In Japan, things proceed in a slow, roundabout way, yet the general direction of change offers unmistakable parallels to trends in both the Anglo-Saxon and the European world.

11

If the heyday of Pierpont Morgan represented the high-water mark of what we now (ironically) term the "European model" of a banker-dominated economy, then the Wall Street of the 1980s embodied, in a pure, distilled form, the "American model" of a stock market–based economy. For old-school bankers, the 1980s—with their raiders and junk bonds, greenmailers and asset-strippers—characterized everything they had dreaded would come to pass with the demise of relationship banking. Every company abruptly seemed a plaything of the stock market, a potential takeover target, subject to the caprices of investors, money managers, leveraged-buyout firms, and takeover artists. As the bull market that started in 1982 careened from one merger to the next, the takeover chain seemed endless and self-perpetuating. By the time the melee was over, many companies were freighted with crippling debt, many plants had been closed, and many workers fired to service that debt. From a historic standpoint, the Grand Guignol proved there were worse things than companies controlled by sleek, fiery tycoons with a proprietary hold over their clients.

Fortunately, there were some compensating features to the mayhem. Blown to smithereens was the old clubhouse world that had bound corporate managers, directors, and bankers in a tacit conspiracy against the public. Instead, the principle was irreversibly established that companies were answerable to shareholders and had to meet universal performance requirements. If many raiders were selfish, destructive men, aiming for the quick kill and heedless of consequences, they at least banished complacency from the executive suite and hastened long-overdue economic restructuring. At least some of America's competitive verve in the 1990s probably stems from the terror of stock-market predators in the 1980s. Every CEO in America must now ponder the stock price of his company as a daily verdict on his performance and a possible prophecy of the length of his tenure. Farewell to the days of patient, passive investors.

The new stock-market ascendancy has some decided drawbacks. It may well account for much of the current myopia that afflicts corporate executives, who must answer to their new taskmasters, the shareholders. Both small and large investors, applying the same standards to all publicly traded companies, are impatient for results and overly quick to punish laggards. Their restlessness helps to clean out corporate deadwood and is certainly an antidote to managerial complacency, but it also produces a deadly short-term orientation. Boosting profits and productivity can take time, whereas costs can always be brutally cut by firing masses of workers and shutting plants. Pressed by investors, too many corporate managers are now resorting to the fast fix and gimmicky solution—the bloodbath known as "downsizing" being a prime example—instead of the creative long-term growth strategy. All too many chief executives seem to manage their stock price rather than their company. I can only suppose that, like Keynes, they assume that, in the long run, we are all contentedly dead and should therefore focus on near-term results.

As mentioned earlier, Wall Street bankers had long insulated management from shareholder pressure by enforcing a taboo on hostile takeovers. They were the fiercely protective gatekeepers who kept out the barbarian hordes. In part this was an unintentional by-product of the system of exclusive client relations. Investment bankers feared that one captive client might ask them to raid another, forcing them to choose and sacrifice one of the two accounts. For a long time, they didn't mind forgoing fees for mergers and acquisitions. In the early postwar era, basic underwriting remained so profitable that investment bankers relegated mergers-and-acquisitions work to a lowly place. During the 1960s, they still sometimes dispensed merger advice gratis, as a lagniappe to keep open the pipeline of profitable underwriting business. For the investment banker, underwriting remained the essence of relationship banking, just as wholesale lending was for the commercial banker. During the 1970s, as described earlier, the immemorial reasons for shunning takeover work disappeared. Once-tractable corporate treasurers began to flex their muscles and defy their traditional bankers, playing off one against another. Even at Morgan Stanley, the golden chains of exclusivity were smashed when IBM brought in Salomon Brothers as a co-manager in 1979. Once investment bankers had to compete for deals on the basis of price, underwriting became a humdrum commodity business with minuscule profit margins, hastening the shift from "relationship" to "transactional" banking. And profit margins on underwriting have continued to plunge inexorably in the 1990s, falling far below the returns earned by pedestrian retail brokers. To return to our bar graph, this has come about because the providers and consumers of capital have become more powerful in the postwar era than the historic middleman, the banker.

With their traditional business in decline and client links eroding (of late even start-up companies have had the nerve to dump their underwriters right after their initial public offerings) fancy Wall Street houses had to cast about for a new revenue source and found it by serving as high-priced strategists and razzle-dazzle dealmakers in the 1980s. Where they had previously been Establishment guardians, parrying threats to management, they now played the role of outsiders, storming the executive suites. If still "investment bankers," they belonged to a separate species altogether. Having repudiated their urbane, genteel ways, they exhibited a taste for blood sport and dropped Gregory Peck as their role model, substituting Sylvester Stallone. Where Wall Street bankers had been studiously low-key, operating invisibly behind closed doors, the new breed thrived on publicity and were sometimes as prominent in the newspapers as the raiders they advised. For their services, they picked up multimillion-dollar fees that eclipsed any money available in underwriting. They also grafted two lucrative sidelines on to their merger work: providing temporary "bridge" loans to finance takeovers and issuing junk bonds, which offered much richer margins than conventional bonds. In short, the takeover wars of the 1980s proved a godsend for Wall Street, then frantically searching for substitutes as corporations outgrew their historic bankers. All the Wall Street glitz of the 1980s but thinly masked the fact that bankers had lost their secure business of providing financing for large businesses.

The takeover binge of the 1980s was driven in part by the availability of money—both commercial bank loans and junk bonds. Cash was the steady oxygen flow that energized the boom, pumping up small raiders to legendary proportions. And why did the commercial banks have so much to lend? The answer is that, as in Germany and Japan, they had been orphaned by their corporate clients. In the 1970s, their best blue-chip clients had begun to pass on them for loans and head for the capital markets, issuing the short-term promissory notes known as "commercial paper." It was this dissolution of their core corporate business that seduced commercial banks in the 1980s into all manner of financial folly, especially the disastrous loans to commercial property developers. Once considered a taboo, illiquid form of lending, property loans came to account for a third of the total loan book of some large banks. Bereft of direction, commercial banks rushed into one lending fad after another, including Latin American lending and leveraged buyout loans, with the strange abandon of the damned.

Over the last twenty years, American commercial banks have acquired a hollowed-out feel as their wholesale lending business has melted away. In many banking conglomerates that cater to large companies, the traditional lending business is a minor, dwindling portion of their total product mix, with the portion of income derived from the interest spread between deposits and loans dipping further each year; Citibank, for instance, now collects only 50 percent of its revenue from interest payments as it segues into fee-based services. To offset this loss, commercial banks have become more deeply involved in the capital markets that stole away their primary clients in the first place. In the retail banking world, they have bundled loans—whether for mortgage payments or credit-card receivables—into securities that can be marketed and traded like bonds. Such "securitization" has blurred the line between lending and underwriting, rendering it meaningless. A growing portion of commercial-bank profits comes from trading securities, dealing in foreign exchange, offering derivatives and other hedging instruments, selling insurance and mutual funds, and offering credit cards.

To the extent allowed by law, commercial banks are now metamorphosing into universal banks. Stymied by Congressional cowardice and inaction, federal regulators, on a selective basis, have allowed bank holding companies to cross the New Deal line and underwrite securities on a restricted basis. In early April 1977, Bankers Trust swallowed up Alex. Brown, a Baltimore-based securities house, in a move that seemed to presage the imminent fusion of many other banks and brokerage firms. Glass-Steagall is dying the death of a thousand lashes and informed observers pre-dict its total repeal by 1998 at the latest. Bankers, brokers, and in-surance agents now seem resigned to the ultimate convergence of their businesses into a single, all-encompassing financial services industry. For the first time since the days of Pierpont Morgan, it is even conceivable that Congress will tear down the barrier be-tween commerce and finance and allow banks to own industrial companies, or be owned by them.

Nevertheless, with straight underwriting about as profitable as wholesale lending, banks no longer lobby for the repeal of Glass-Steagall with any particular urgency. As more commercial banks enter underwriting, profits are being pounded to the van-ishing point, promising that the total repeal of Glass-Steagall, when it comes, will be a Pyrrhic victory. A cynic might well say that as the commercial bankers now come crashing through the front door of the mansion, the investment bankers are fleeing out the back, convinced that the house is pretty worthless. In all like-lihood, the commercial bankers will use their newly won powers after the repeal of Glass-Steagall to shore up their presence in re-tail brokerage rather than try to dominate stock and bond under-writing.

To return to the investment-banking side of Wall Street. In the 1980s it seemed that the investment banks had found in merger work a lucrative oasis from which they could never be dislodged, but they celebrated too soon. Do you remember that old song with the refrain "Anything you can do I can do better"? The lyric conveys the skeptical attitude blue-ribbon companies increas-ingly adopt toward Wall Street bankers. A conspicuous trend of late has been the tendency of companies to conduct their own takeovers, dispensing with investment bankers. By the mid-1990s, more than a quarter of merger deals around the globe were being handled without the assistance of high-priced financial advisers. This sharp demotion of the investment banker's role has been carefully masked because many companies seal their deals by having Wall Street firms issue "fairness opinions," certifying that a reasonable price has been paid for a company. For this routine work, investment banks receive only a pittance, yet for public-relations purposes, they add the dollar amount of such deals into their mergers-and-acquisitions totals for the year, inflating the figures. Early in the century, corporate managers were often rough-hewn, self-made men, with little financial sophistication. Nowadays, the upper ranks of corporate management are chock-a-block with lawyers, accountants, and MBAs who feel, after a few takeover battles, that they know as much or more than their bankers. It's another sign that corporations which once slavishly genuflected before their Wall Street bankers no longer feel the need to bother with them.

That bankers have surrendered their banking monopoly to their clients is evident everywhere on the financial scene today. Many companies once subservient to the House of Morgan and other elite investment houses have become sizable financial firms in their own right. General Motors sells insurance, makes loans, and issues mortgages. General Electric Capital Corporation heads a growing life-insurance empire and is a major issuer of commercial paper. IBM is deeply involved in home-banking and electronic-payments systems while AT&T issues credit cards. For five of the past six years, Ford Motor has actually made more money as a banker than as a car maker. The list could be expanded indefinitely. What makes these companies rugged competitors for even the most robust banks is that they possess top credit ratings—usually far superior to the banks'—can raise capital for expansion at low cost, and operate with few regulatory restraints. It is the old story of banking emerging spontaneously from successful commerce. Many "non-banks" that have bedeviled banks in recent years started out as industrial companies.

Anyone who doubts the freedom of blue-chip companies

from their bankers should ponder the stockpiles of cash held by major American companies by the end of 1996. After several years of frenzied expansion, Microsoft had $9 billion in cash and short-term investments while Intel had $8.2 billion. The Big Three automakers, who long enriched Wall Street coffers, were sitting on staggering piles of cash: $17 billion for General Motors, $15.4 billion for Ford Motor, and $7.8 billion for Chrysler. By late 1996 the liquid assets of all American companies outside the financial services sector had reached an extraordinary $679 billion as many American companies replicated the good fortune that Standard Oil had enjoyed a century before and become ersatz banks.

At this point in my argument, some skeptical readers are doubtless smirking. If the situation for the Wall Street firms is as gloomy as the author contends, why are they expanding so fast worldwide? Why do I keep reading about young hotshots pulling down multimillion-dollar salaries? Surely the banker can't be a dying breed if so many people are making so much money? The objection is a perfectly legitimate one. Nobody is being crucified or martyred on Wall Street. Firms such as Morgan Stanley and Goldman, Sachs are riding high, expanding around the globe, and booking record profits, and they seem anything but sickly. Even the commercial banks reaped a record $51 billion in profit for 1996—a fifth consecutive year of record profits. Hardly the results that would seem the occasion for my mournful requiem.

Well, right here I should beat my breast, shout mea culpa, and sheepishly make a confession. For the sake of accuracy, I should have entitled my essay "The Death of Banking" instead of "The Death of the Banker." For bankers have prospered mightily as they have cast off banking business in favor of other financial services. Both by instinct and long-range design, the smartest banks have explored and responded to the crisis I am describing here. Sensitive to the altered power relationships, investment banks have shifted emphasis away from straight stock-and-bond underwriting, just as commercial banks such as J.P. Morgan & Company and Bankers Trust have all but scrapped wholesale lending. While some underwriting niches remain extremely profitable—especially junk bonds, initial public offerings, and other forms of financing that primarily cater to smaller and medium-sized firms without access to the capital markets—the conventional middleman tasks of underwriting and wholesale lending have contracted inside these conglomerates.

To surmount the crisis, such firms, as a rule, have ceased to behave as bankers—that is, as financial intermediaries. Fee-based work is increasingly vital to them, especially advising foreign governments on privatizations. They make some money from brokerage commissions, especially those with retail networks. They have mostly succeeded, however, by transforming themselves into capital providers who engage in a vast amount of "proprietary" trading for their own account, whether in stocks, bonds, futures, options, or foreign currencies. They have created huge buyout funds where they invest their own money alongside private pension funds, university endowments, and other institutions, taking stakes in companies as passive or active investors. Perhaps their fastest-growing area is portfolio management, where they manage money for others or administer their own mutual funds. In all these investment banks, vast numbers of people—including traders, salesmen, and research analysts—provide services to institutional and retail investors, pampering them as corporate clients were once given the royal treatment in an earlier era. Going back to our bar graph, we can see the whole financial landscape shifting drastically toward the capital providers. Tiny at the start of the century, the institutional investors now tower over the world of money. Without further ado, we should move on to examine these new arbiters of the financial universe: the mutual funds.

12

*T*o the tycoons of J. P. Morgan's day, it would have seemed an absurd pipedream, even a shameful comedown, to imagine that at some misty future time the cumulative savings of tens of millions of small Main Street investors would constitute the main pool of Wall Street capital. Yet in the space of a century, the retail world of finance has overtaken the wholesale world of Wall Street: the peasantry have burst through the gates, overrunning the palace grounds. Small investors have gone from being minor participants, eternal suckers of the stock market, to being the motive force behind rallies. As an atomized group, the "little people" could never have wielded this influence, but banded together in mutual funds, they have now inverted the whole hierarchy of Wall Street power.

Behind this shift lies a demographic revolution. Investing has always been a matter of placing bets about the future, and we now have a much longer future to envision. A century ago, medical science often seemed just one step ahead of quackery and could cure relatively few infectious diseases; many workers simply dropped dead in harness and had little incentive to budget for retirement. As life expectancy lengthened, however, creating long retirements and populating the state of Florida, corporations and governments both assumed some of the burden for supporting the graying population. During the past decade, as the baby-boom generation has entered middle age, it has succumbed to deep anxiety—now sharpening, I think, into full-blown panic—about how to foot the bills for old age. In my view, this anxiety reflects three mutually reinforcing doubts. People wonder whether an overextended welfare state can support an aging population at existing funding levels; whether corporations can maintain adequate retirement programs in a harshly competitive global environment;

and whether medical insurance can keep pace with the exorbitant cost of new medical technologies. At least one response to these worries has been a thunderous stampede of small investors into the stock market. Once upon a time, retirement investments were invariably stodgy and safe. After inflation in the 1970s destroyed faith in bank accounts and long-term bonds, and deflation in the late 1980s did the same for real estate, the Stock Exchange, by default, turned into a souped-up, turbocharged national retirement plan—with consequences as yet unknown. Investors are now tolerating a level of risk in their retirement accounts that would have been considered unthinkable by trust-fund managers a few decades ago.

During the early postwar years, most American corporations funded workers' pensions through defined benefit plans that were managed by institutional investors, placing the onus of performance on the corporation itself. In the 1980s and 1990s, corporate America decided that it was more economical and infinitely more soothing to set up defined contribution plans that place the entire burden of risk on the individual beneficiary. The amount of money in the new defined contribution plans now amounts to $1.5 trillion, or slightly more than the $1.4 trillion in the old defined benefit plans. This has put tens of millions of Americans in the alternately giddy and terrifying position of managing their own retirement money without any realistic sense of the market's historic performance. After six straight years of a nearly vertical liftoff in the stock market indices, many of these investors had little appreciation that the stock market was not a one-way rocket ride to the moon but a wild roller coaster that carries investors through exhilarating upturns and sickening downturns.

Let me cite numbers that will give some tiny inkling of the magnitude of the burgeoning American mutual-fund boom, for these piles of cash make the Morgan and Rothschild fortunes look like petty change in comparison. In 1986, 1,840 mutual funds controlled $716 billion in stock, bond, and money-market assets, and a decade later the number had mushroomed to more than 7,000 funds, possessing $3.7 trillion in assets. This amount is rapidly approaching the $4.6 trillion of total assets lodged in America's 10,000 commercial banks. Indeed, much of the money that has flowed into mutual funds in recent years has resulted from a wholesale raid on bank deposits. At the current, vertiginous rate of growth—about 32 percent per annum—mutual funds will shortly supersede the banking system as the chief repository of American household savings. In 1980 only about 6 percent of American households had dabbled in mutual funds; by 1995, nearly one-third had taken the plunge, with the number still growing as mutual-fund investments are incorporated into more and more retirement plans. In 1996 Americans channeled a record $235 billion into mutual funds, at a torrid rate of about $20 billion per month. Between September 1990 and March 1996, stock mutual funds added $531.5 billion to their portfolios—or three times the amount that had been invested in all such funds between 1924, when the first mutual fund, the Massachusetts Investors Trust, was created, and August 1990.

A century ago, the Stock Exchange was seen as the shady lair of professional speculators and sharpers, a place as wicked as a pool hall or gambling den, and certainly no place for decent, God-fearing folk. Now, as the middle-class fascination with stocks has blossomed into a storybook romance, set to strings, the market has shed whatever stigma it once had. From about 1.5 million at the time of the 1929 Crash, the number of stock and mutual-fund investors leaped to 6 million in the early 1950s, to 20 million in the 1960s, and to more than 63 million today. Of those 63 million, 25 million have entered the market during the past four, frenetic, highly atypical years. The stock market has come to seem a safe and wholesome place for the whole family, much as Las Vegas, once the louche hideaway for gangsters and their molls, is now a cherished Sunday destination for Granny and the bridge club. Stock investing has become a hallowed American spectator sport, as comfortably mainstream as Coca-Cola, Wal-Mart, or Disneyland. For veterans of the old rigged stock market, with its ruthless pools, treacherous corners, and vicious bear raids, Wall Street today seems much too clean-cut and respectable, having sacrificed the spice of sin.

Nowadays it is hard to remember that much of American history once revolved around vituperative debates between Wall Street and Main Street, creditors and debtors, rich people who favored hard money and low inflation and working people who fretted about jobs and growth. Main Street can no longer clash too vigorously with Wall Street since the two sides have grown indistinguishable with the rise of giant brokerage chains and mutual-funds groups. Many ordinary Americans have developed the classic reflexes of creditors, unwittingly internalizing the values of early-twentieth-century moguls. They brood about inflation far more than unemployment and applaud the tight-money policies of the Federal Reserve Board in a way once restricted to the polo set. As they cheer for their stocks and mutual funds, they identify with the interests of corporate America as never before.

If you scan the many magazines now devoted to personal finance, you will find listed hundreds of mutual funds, giving the impression of a highly fragmented, almost anarchic industry, the last haven for individualists. Yet the industry has already undergone considerable consolidation, with the top five fund groups hoarding more than a third of the industry's wealth. As of November 1996, the assets of these five financial dreadnoughts ranked as follows: Fidelity ($431 billion in assets), Vanguard ($244 billion), Capital Research ($175 billion), Merrill Lynch ($160 billion), and Franklin/Templeton ($134 billion). In a 1996 survey of the money-management industry, Goldman, Sachs flatly predicted that, within five years, the industry would be governed by twenty to twenty-five giant firms, each with a war chest of at least $150 billion in assets, and one suspects that the prophecy will come true long before then.

If I can play the soothsayer for the moment, I would wager that, during the next generation, the world of finance will be completely reorganized around these leviathans and the large retail brokerage chains—the two major conduits for the retirement money pourinig into the stock market. As gigantic suppliers of capital, mutual funds are already taking over the capital-allocation functions once exercised by bankers in an age of scarce capital. Consider the riches of Fidelity Investments, the parent of the flagship Magellan Fund, with more than 10 million customers. In a preview of things to come, Fidelity has relentlessly expanded into underwriting, brokerage, insurance, and credit cards and has even struck a strategic alliance to distribute stocks underwritten by Salomon Brothers. In this transformation, the middle bar of our three-pronged graph—that of the financial intermediary—becomes subordinate to the capital providers or even disappears altogether in the face of direct contacts between companies and investors.

Given the soaring growth of mutual funds, one is entitled to wonder whether fund managers will qualify as the new financial barons of the twenty-first century, much like the Rothschilds in the nineteenth century or the Morgans in the early twentieth century. The case is a superficially plausible one. As custodians of phenomenal wealth, these people supervise portfolios worth tens of billions of dollars and take home millions of dollars in compensation. Corporate executives fear them more than they do swashbuckling raiders and think twice before refusing to return their phone calls. With this do-or-die power over companies, some fund managers may be forgiven for yielding to momentary delusions of grandeur. They have become the de facto private planners of our economy, shifting capital on a minute-to-minute basis. Much of the buoyancy of the American economy in the 1990s probably comes from their patent bias toward rapid growth and technological innovation—preferences for which the more stolid traditional bankers were never famous.

Having said that, I think that one can easily overstate the power of these financial functionaries. Instead of being lords of the market, they are really slaves to a punishing arithmetic, enjoying a circumscribed power. Fund managers inhabit a fishbowl world where everything is quantified, objectified, and published; a J. P. Morgan could blunder in privacy for years. Each morning's newspaper lists the net asset value of all funds, thus subjecting these managers—like the corporate executives they monitor—to a universal performance standard. If they fall behind in the race, they are quickly cashiered, for apart from their ability to deliver superior performance, they have no independent source of power. Given the ease of comparing results and shifting assets among these largely standardized products, the mutual-fund business can only operate successfully as a meritocracy. Investors care about rates of return, not personalities, and usually don't even know the names of the people who manage their money. The power of a J. P. Morgan today isn't vested in mutual-fund managers, but parceled out among millions of small investors who follow their stocks and mutual funds and transfer money, in an instant, from places of lower to higher returns. These impatient, unsentimental "little people" are the true martinets of modern finance.

In its formative years, the mutual-fund industry managed to produce the occasional superstar, such as Peter Lynch, but he was the exception who proved the rule. More and more fund managers are submerged in a vast, impersonal mechanism as they struggle with growing amounts of wealth. The great mutual funds are like superships that find it difficult to maneuver in choppy seas. The more they succeed, the more investors reward them with cash; the greater these inflows, the more difficult they find it to outperform the market, or even match their own past performance. This syndrome will turn many young hotshots on Wall Street into worn-out hacks before their time. More and more, we are witnessing the pathetic, futile spectacle of money managers trying to beat the herd when, as should be obvious, they *are* the herd. In 1996, the average money manager's stock picks rose 22.8 percent, or exactly the same amount as the Standard & Poor's 500-stock index, while in 1995, the average money manager actually lagged the index.

The performance sweepstakes may also push portfolio managers into taking excessive risk, lest they seem inept or old-fashioned compared with their speculative, higher-yielding, competitors. Unlike bankers, mutual-fund managers have no legal obligation to return the original principal to investors and can gamble accordingly. During periods when the stock market is rising sharply, the mutual-fund manager is under excruciating pressure to stay fully invested, even against his better judgment, and can be unwillingly caught up in the collective mayhem. So far from necessarily introducing safety and the manager's more mature judgment into the market, the mutual funds, in a rampaging bull market, can become dangerous accomplices in a competitive, speculative dynamic. No mutual-fund manager can long escape the quiet, daily tyranny of the numbers and may be forced to mimic the high risk–high reward profile of competitors if he wishes to retain his assets.

The triumph of the small investor is directly related to the plethora of information now available about companies. The old Wall Street banks, those marble temples of mystery, were chary of giving out information and rebuffed inquiries from the press. As private partnerships, they felt no obligation to justify their decisions to the world and freely traded on inside information about their clients, to the detriment of the public. Afraid of giving their rivals any competitive edge, corporations also jealously guarded information about their operations, tried to reveal as little about themselves as possible, and showed scant regard for the average investor.

On the new Wall Street, everything occurs out in the open. Any financial system based on the stock market is bound to be as transparent as the old bank-based system was opaque, so that it is fitting that asset managers operate in glass skyscrapers. The financial world today is swamped with a nearly indigestible amount of information. Besides reams of annual reports, prospectuses, and registration statements, investors are deluged with information from newsletters, the business press, rating agencies, brokerage-house analysts, and cable channels that cover the stock market from opening to closing bell. The stock market has generated an all-encompassing information culture to evaluate the performance of company executives and mutual-fund managers alike. The old wholesale banker has been stripped of his most powerful prerogative: his monopoly over corporate information, which is now instantaneously and impartially transmitted to investors around the world.

13

The mutual-fund boom now sweeping through Wall Street has become a whirlwind threatening to topple the entire structure of investment and commercial banking. In February 1997, the tony Morgan Stanley shocked the financial world by announcing a merger with the distinctly unstylish Dean Witter, forging a new and all but unpronounceable entity called Morgan Stanley, Dean Witter, Discover. For more than sixty years, Morgan Stanley had epitomized the blue-blooded, aristocratic, Wall Street investment house, engaging in a strictly wholesale business with governments, blue-chip companies, and ultrarich investors and betraying a lordly indifference to small investors. Since the 1920s, Dean Wittter had typified the Main Street world of retail brokerage, with 8,500 brokers dispersed across the country. It was owned by Sears, Roebuck—the emblem of middle America—in the 1980s and some Dean Witter salesmen had actually hawked stocks from booths set up in Sears department stores. This stupefying marriage was something akin to the duchess suddenly eloping with the footman and promised a culture clash of epic proportions.

The new firm instantly leapfrogged ahead of Merrill Lynch to become the world's largest securities firm. Even before the merger, Morgan Stanley had ranked first in global mergers and acquisitions, third in global underwriting, and fourth in institutional fund management. By teaming up with Dean Witter, it would now boast $33 billion in capital and a market capitalization of $21 billion while serving 3.2 million retail investors, 7 million mutual-fund investors, and 39 million people holding the Discover card. Beyond the bricks-and-mortar network of Dean Witter offices, the merger would also give Morgan Stanley access to investors who favored Internet trading through Lombard Brokerage, a Dean Witter subsidiary.

Though this behemoth would not be the world's first large, fully integrated securities firm, straddling the wholesale and retail world—Merrill Lynch claimed that honor—the merger was pregnant with significance because Merrill had branched out from a lowly retail base, while Morgan Stanley had stepped down from its lofty perch in wholesale work. The union wrote the epitaph for the old Wall Street, which for more than a century had revolved around the distinction between wholesale and retail, high and low finance, Wall Street and Main Street. With the Morgan Stanley–Dean Witter fusion, these historic distinctions lost all significance. The mystery-shrouded Wall Street houses that had once ruled railroads and heavy industry and dealt with foreign governments, breeding a thousand conspiracy myths in the American heartland, was now about to vanish.

Just three years before, Morgan Stanley had been angling to merge with S.G. Warburg & Co. in London, banking everything on its push into global, wholesale investment banking. Now, in a stunning strategic turnabout, it was staking its future on domestic expansion, underlining the overriding importance of retail distribution outlets. To return one last time to our tripartite bar graph, the providers of capital, both institutional and individual investors, had irrevocably established their supremacy, turning the historic structure of Wall Street topsy-turvy. We should mention two other factors behind Morgan Stanley's decision to truckle to the proletariat. Its traditional corporate clients, who had once tamely submitted to exclusive relations with the firm, were now rich and independent, often sitting atop huge cash hoards. And Morgan Stanley executives had experienced persistent frustration with their relatively low share price, which reflected investor discomfort with the firm's dependence on volatile securities business. In the old days of the stuffy Wall Street partnerships, these year-to-year fluctuations didn't bother the well-heeled owners, but stock market investors are less forgiving and prefer regular, predictable growth. Like the companies it has long advised, Morgan Stanley has itself become a creature of the stock market, forced to do its bidding and dance to the tune of millions of small investors.

It now seemed only a matter of time before the other investment banks would pair off with brokerage firms or mutual-funds groups; for this reason the Morgan Stanley–Dean Witter merger perhaps delivered the coup de grâce to Glass-Steagall. By strengthening the competitive edge of the investment banks, these new partnerships seemed calculated to weaken their longstanding resistance to repeal of the act. By the same token, the commercial banks were now desperately eager to grab the remaining retail conduits to market their own families of mutual funds. All in all, the Morgan Stanley–Dean Witter merger signalled the long-heralded convergence of the banking, brokerage, and even insurance industries into a single, all-encompassing financial services industry.

14

*I*f J. P. Morgan were abruptly resurrected at the corner of Broad and Wall, amid a huge puff of satanic cigar smoke, and strolled down the street, poking his bulbous nose into banks and brokerage houses, how would he react? First, he would be amazed at how many banks had fled uptown, following their clients. Then, he would be appalled at how his discreet, private mandarin world had been taken over by vulgarians. He would wonder at the vast trading rooms, the legions of salesmen and analysts, all the people oriented toward the noisy Stock Exchange. He would be aghast at the unseemly bustle, the frantically competitive atmosphere, the wheeling and dealing between companies and investors who felt no need to heed the dictation of their bankers.

If a big black limousine materialized and whisked Morgan off to Times Square, he would stare agog at the new world headquarters of Morgan Stanley, a descendant of his own House of Morgan. First, he would be amazed—then color with embarrassment—to see the name Morgan Stanley splashed across the front of this jazzy new skyscraper. Didn't they remember that self-respecting merchant bankers never posted their names? He would notice—doubtless cringing with horror—that a three-tiered stock ticker ran around the outside of the building, screaming for pedestrians' attention. Where was the dignified understatement? The commitment to secrecy? The proper contempt for the public? Why couldn't they just peddle their mystique, their exclusivity, their snob appeal, as they always had? If he stayed around long enough and barked out enough questions, he would learn that his august name was now plastered across small-town brokerage offices throughout America. As he pondered these strange, unsettling things, Morgan would realize that perhaps he had died at the right moment. Before his shade returned to the other side—leaving behind just a telltale wisp of cigar smoke—he would sadly conclude that at the end of the twentieth century he had become a ghost in more than one sense.

TYCOONS I:

J. Pierpont Morgan

*A*s we attend funeral rites for the old Wall Street, it would perhaps be an appropriate moment to honor its memory by returning to its origins. The House of Morgan was the principal carrier of the merchant-banking culture that originated in the City of London. Since Britain had long been riddled with class distinctions, the behavior of its elite banks seemed fully consistent with the aloof, private ways of its upper class. In America, by contrast, the wholesale banks, steadfastly barred to small investors, seemed an alien bloom grafted onto the native stock of an officially egalitarian culture. The top-hatted money men with their striped pants and superior manners defied the friendly, open, backslapping culture of a largely agrarian country. It therefore comes as no surprise that the man who personified this transplanted London culture, John Pierpont Morgan, attracted much of the xenophobia, rural discontent, and populist rage of his day.

In pondering Morgan's peripatetic boyhood, it is hard to resist the suspicion that he was being groomed, from an early age, by a considerate fate, to assume his appointed place at the apex of Anglo-American finance. His background, his sympathies, his in-

terests, his family—all seemed expressly designed to groom him
for his commanding post astride the massive flow of capital between London and New York in the late nineteenth century. On
the one hand, the roots of his life reached into the Yankee trading
soil of Puritan New England. His grandfather Joseph Morgan was
a thriving Hartford businessman, a lusty hymn-singer and Bible-
thumper, who invested in canals, railroads, hotels, steamboats,
and insurance companies. After serving as a partner in merchant
houses in Hartford and Boston, Pierpont's father, Junius Spencer
Morgan—a stern, grim-visaged man who seems to glower at us
from the few extant photographs of him—became a junior partner
of George Peabody's London bank in 1854. A Massachusetts native, Peabody had made a fortune in London selling American
state-government and railroad securities to often restive, dubious
British investors. A bloodless, pathological pinchpenny, he could
have served as a model for Dickens's Scrooge. Late in his career,
however, his fortune safely in hand, he experienced a spiritual
conversion, decided to cleanse his hands of the taint of banking,
and emerged as a sainted figure of Victorian philanthropy. As part
of this valedictory to the sublunary world of affairs, he left his
bank to Junius Morgan.

So J. Pierpont Morgan spent his boyhood on both sides of the
Atlantic, reflecting his father's Anglo-American odyssey. Pierpont
attended school in Hartford and Boston, and then, as an adolescent, studied in Switzerland and Germany, spending vacations
with his family in London. He absorbed British culture into his
bloodstream, visiting Buckingham Palace, sitting through ser-
mons at Saint Paul's, and fondling a million pounds of gold bul-
lion at the Bank of England. At a time when most young
Americans were provincial hayseeds, Pierpont had a cosmopolitan air. As an adult, he would identify strongly with both British
and American culture, never feeling an incompatibility between
them. Unlike most Americans, he didn't mistrust European roy-
alty or rebel against the presumed decadence of European society.

In our hubris, we tend to fancy that global markets are modern inventions, by-products of advanced computer technology, whereas the world was already crisscrossed with capital flows by the mid nineteenth century. The first Latin American debt crisis was well under way in the 1820s. As mentioned earlier, London merchant bankers tended to gaze outward and grew so enamored of the excellent returns on investments in North America, Latin America, and the Far East that they were constantly faulted for neglecting British industry. Instead of blanketing the British interior with branch offices, the most prestigious houses went abroad to set up interlocking partnerships in the main overseas capitals. Members of the *haute banque* caste typically sent their sons abroad to serve apprenticeships with affiliated banks, then steered them into sound dynastic marriages to spread the family influence.

When Junius dispatched his son, Pierpont, to Wall Street in 1857, he merely emulated the Rothschilds and other regnant dynasties of the day. Briefly, Pierpont served as partner in the firm of Duncan Sherman, where he was supposed to play a self-effacing role and humbly learn the rudiments of the trade. But this broad-chested, rambunctious young man, then twenty, seemed fully formed, with a preternatural faith in his own judgment. His mind was strong, if not always subtle, and he never seemed to vacillate over decisions, which took shape in a great rush of judgment. With J. Pierpont Morgan, the wish was always father to the deed, as if his brain's wiring bypassed the higher reasoning powers. In 1859, while in New Orleans on business, he learned that a boatload of Brazilian coffee had arrived without a buyer. Confident he could find buyers, he risked the entire capital of Duncan, Sherman by buying and reselling the coffee shipment. The deal, however profitable, unnerved his older and less daring partners—probably the reason Pierpont's relations with them rapidly cooled and he failed to make partner.

In 1861, he departed to start his own shop, J.P. Morgan & Company. During the Civil War, he bought and sold securities, gambled in the frenzied gold pits, and brokered grain and British iron. He also financed a questionable arms deal, extending a $20,000 loan to one Simon Stevens, who bought 5,000 obsolete carbines from the Union government, rifled these smooth-bore weapons, then sold them back to the government three months later at six times the original price. Exactly how much Pierpont knew about this sordid deal has been exhaustively debated. What seems incontrovertible is that he didn't spend the Civil War brooding about preserving the Union or emancipating the slaves, but looked to enrich himself during the bloodshed. He hired a substitute to fight in his place—a common enough practice among members of his socioeconomic class—and whimsically referred to this doppelgänger as "the other J. P. Morgan."

Before long, Junius Morgan suspected—probably with equal parts fear and admiration—that he had a bull-headed young prodigy on his hands. From across the Atlantic, he proceeded to pound conservative precepts into this strong-willed, wayward young man, droning on about the need for caution in all dealings. While he often chafed at this restraining hand, Pierpont revered his father and respected his judgment. Probably his paramount duty was to gather Wall Street intelligence for Junius. Twice a week, with unvarying punctuality, he sat down and composed lengthy letters to him, providing comprehensive accounts of financial and political events. Pierpont treasured this correspondence, which he collected into leather-bound volumes; then unaccountably, in 1911, two years before his death, he burned the entire set. This magnificent bonfire obliterated what would have been a historical treasure: a candid, interior glimpse of Anglo-American financial relations extending over a period of more than three decades.

That Morgan torched these sacred letters suggests not only their controversial nature and his possible fear of public exposure—he was already under relentless government investigation—but the integral place of intelligence in nineteenth-century banking. The point is worth stating again: knowledge in those days was as precious as capital. We have already noted the vast information culture that sustains the stock market today. In the old days of mystery and dignity, however, such information had to be laboriously gathered by the bankers themselves. Most companies were family-owned or closely held and even publicly traded firms weren't compelled by regulators to publish information, the main ambition of most executives being to guard the company from outside scrutiny. One skimpy Morgan prospectus for the New York Central Railroad in the 1870s stated, with no trace of irony, "The credit and status of the company are so well known, that it is scarcely necessary to make any public statement." When J.P. Morgan & Company floated International Harvester in 1902, Morgan partner George W. Perkins proudly sent its maiden report to President Roosevelt, boasting that "so far as I know, this is the first instance on record that a corporation, on offering its securities to the public, has given to the public complete information as to its affairs." A banker, of course, knew the state of his own client companies, but he had to make informed guesses about the solvency of prospective clients and correspondent banks, which meant constantly digging for information.

Right before he died, Pierpont Morgan testified grudgingly before the Pujo hearings in Washington. This was a sensational probe into a quasimythical Money Trust on Wall Street, supposedly masterminded by Morgan. Morgan, of course, regarded such inquiries as patent harassment—a pesky swarm of fleas around his elephantine presence—and his testimony consisted largely of contemptuous grimaces and monosyllabic grunts. At several points, however, while being mercilessly questioned by counsel Samuel Untermyer, Morgan deigned to utter some complete English sentences, even minted a few epigrammatic statements, as in the following celebrated exchange:

Untermyer: Is not commercial credit based primarily upon money or property?

Morgan: No, sir, the first thing is character.

Untermyer: Before money or property?

Morgan: Before money or anything else. Money cannot buy it . . . Because a man I do not trust could not get money from me on all the bonds in Christendom.

This declaration was roundly cheered by businessmen, even if it prompted derisory guffaws from reformers. It certainly sounded as if Morgan were giving a sanctimonious veneer to what some would call plain cronyism. Yet perhaps the good reason here was, in fact, the real reason. Handicapped by limited information, bankers needed speedy ways to size people up and often relied on quick intuitions in the absence of hard data. Character was a short cut to determining credit-worthiness, and clients often searched for comparable clues about the personal rectitude of their bankers. In 1904, the German sociologist Max Weber, touring the American South, was startled to see a local banker submit to baptism in an icy stream. When asked the reason for this, he was told that the banker had to establish his bona fides, not with the Lord, but with depositors, who felt more confident leaving money with a devout Baptist. At a time when swindles were legion, honest information was the coin of the realm. Since it was often hard to verify reports about distant railroad, canal, or mining ventures—the readers of Trollope's fine novel *The Way We Live Now* will recall how a large portion of the London aristocracy was duped about a rail project in North America—the promoter's character was often the one surefire clue to the venture's soundness.

By the standards of self-made American entrepreneurs, the Morgans represented "old money." Nonetheless, Junius lacked a fortune sufficient to found a financial empire and had to cast about for strategic alliances to plump up his capital. Blessed with considerable luck and talent, he managed to commandeer two other family fortunes for that purpose. When George Peabody retired in 1864, he reneged on a long-standing agreement that would have allowed Junius Morgan to retain the use of his capital and name. (Had Peabody not demanded the deletion of his name, the House of Morgan would today be the House of Peabody.) This shabby, duplicitous treatment undercut Peabody's claim to new-found sanctity, yet the curmudgeon's reversion to form shouldn't blind us to the fact that something rare in banking circles had occurred. Here was a childless bachelor (at least if one obligingly ignores the mistress and illegitimate daughter Peabody had tucked away in Brighton) who handed over control of a prospering London bank to someone outside his family. This placed the Morgans in the exceedingly nice position of inheriting somebody else's empire on a platter.

With exquisite timing, Junius Morgan succeeded in kidnapping a second great fortune in 1871 by striking an advantageous deal with Anthony J. Drexel of Philadelphia, whose family bank ranked second only to that of Jay Cooke in financing operations for the U.S. government. Aware of Philadelphia's waning power as a financial center, Drexel sought to strengthen his Wall Street connections. The result was a new partnership called Drexel, Morgan & Company, with the order of the names clearly reflecting the importance of the partners. (Morgan didn't drop the Drexel name until 1895, when he christened his firm J.P. Morgan & Company.) Through the Drexel deal, Pierpont became a partner in affiliated Drexel firms in Philadelphia and Paris; along with the houses in New York and London, these interlocking partnerships would constitute the four stars of the Morgan constellation. Through such partnerships, merchant bankers wove together an international financial marketplace that transcended national boundaries and facilitated global trade.

Pierpont Morgan was a gruff, headstrong young man, moody and wilful, who found it difficult to play second fiddle to anyone. If Tony Drexel conferred more capital and prestige on the new union, the young Morgan didn't hesitate to seize control. It is important to note that Pierpont, buffered from his sententious father by the Atlantic Ocean, enjoyed unusual autonomy for a young man and was always accustomed to carrying himself like a boss. He had a terrific head for numbers and snapped out orders in a rapid, staccato style that terrified subordinates. Tutored by his father, he knew the banking business top-to-bottom. As he said in later years, "I can sit down at any clerk's desk, take up his work where he left it and go on with it. . . . I don't like being at any man's mercy." He never depreciated the importance of his father's contribution to his career and punctiliously observed the rites of filial piety. "If I have been able to succeed in the station of life in which I have been cast," he once observed, "I attribute it more than anything to the endorsement of my father's friends."

Almost all of Pierpont Morgan's early exploits revolved around railroads, the main field of competition for wholesale bankers. With their helter-skelter growth after the Civil War, the roads had a voracious appetite for capital, luring British and Continental investors with tantalizing returns that often, in the end, proved a snare and a delusion. As we have seen, many railroads were rife with fraud and corruption and were severely weakened by overbuilding and price wars that forced them to skip dividends; the "London interests" followed events helplessly from afar. Morgan took the latent power in the London shareholdings and activated it to intervene in railroad management. Many outraged British investors had formed bondholder committees to assert their rights, but they needed an agent on the ground, someone who could restore order, an American paladin who would represent their interests and not betray them. The situation required some unique, Anglo-American hybrid and Pierpont Morgan perfectly fit the bill. In Junius's letters, he frequently referred to his son as representing the "London interests," and Pierpont never tired of lecturing arrogant railroad managers that their shareholders wielded final power in their business. "Your roads!" he berated one railroad president. "Your roads belong to my clients!"

Tough and burly, Pierpont wasn't squeamish about doing battle by main force. In 1869, at age thirty-two, he aligned himself with executives of a small upstate New York railroad, the Albany and Susquehanna, who wanted to resist a takeover bid from those ubiquitous rascals of the day, Jay Gould and Jim Fisk. The showdown came at a shareholder meeting on September 7, 1869. According to myth, Morgan barred the husky Fisk from the meeting, flinging him down a steep flight of steps. Whether or not such theatrics occurred, Morgan helped to oust the Gould forces and merge the road with a friendly line, the Delaware and Hudson. In a momentous step, Morgan took a seat on the board of the merged railroad, a signature maneuver that he would duplicate dozens of times until he was universally recognized as czar of more than a third of America's railways.

It is easy to attribute Morgan's power to his titanic personality—the fierce snap judgments, the volcanic temper, the booming voice that shook the rafters. Self-conscious about his disfigured, ruby-red nose, he fixed people with a pitiless gaze if he caught them staring at it. This powder-keg personality could reduce brawny men to heaps of quivering jelly. Yet his imperious nature would have counted for little had the situation not been ripe for banker domination. From our perspective, we can see that the banker was strong because of the weakness of countervailing powers. Had the capital markets been more fully developed, Morgan could never have exercised such dictatorial power over the railroads.

In the late nineteenth century, most company shares were held by family members, directors, and bankers, rather than being broadly distributed among the general public. As a result, the world of mergers and acquisitions had to proceed in decorous, closed-door negotiations—a role for which the private banker, with his tiny partnerships, was ideally suited. As happened with the Albany and Susquehanna, power struggles were continually played out by bankers, directors, lawyers, and judges who remained invisible to the general public. (In the A&S battle, Pierpont owned 600 shares of stock and represented both his own and other interests.) Many skirmishes that the young Morgan engaged in would today take the form of bidding wars on the Stock Exchange floor. In the absence of publicly available information, it would then have been difficult for would-be raiders to form any accurate idea of a company's true value.

In 1879, the swaggering Pierpont, in his early forties, staggered the financial world with an adroit maneuver following the death of Commodore Vanderbilt, America's richest man. Although the Commodore had abused his eldest son and branded him a numbskull, forty-two-year-old William Henry Vanderbilt nonetheless inherited 87 percent of the stock of the New York Central Railroad. It was the young Vanderbilt who achieved instant, if doubtful, immortality with the retort, "The public be damned; I am working for my stockholders." The year 1879 wasn't a very auspicious one to inherit a block of railroad stock. The New York State legislature was holding the Hepburn hearings, which probed collusion between the railroads and Standard Oil. As more and more abuses surfaced, indignant state legislators blustered that they would levy heavy taxes on Vanderbilt's stock. To appease their wrath, Vanderbilt turned to Pierpont Morgan to sell 250,000 shares of his stock. Morgan secured Vanderbilt's agreement to halt all further sales of his stock for a year, or until all the shares had been fully placed. Even with that promise, however, it was problematic whether such a sizable stake could be sold without triggering a precipitous drop in the share price.

In a display of financial legerdemain, Morgan managed to place the entire block without upsetting the stock price and picked up a $3-million commission. He formed a syndicate of powerful financiers, including Jay Gould, Russell Sage, and Cyrus Field, to absorb the shares domestically, but also mobilized his London connections and sold many shares abroad. Once again, Morgan added to his power as well as to his capital, winning a seat on the New York Central board. In hindsight, one is struck by how sedulously Morgan had to scour the globe to find pools of private capital to soak up the stock. An operation of that size taxed the existing markets. If the capital markets had been as deep and liquid as today's, Morgan could have employed the trading desks of dozens of global investment banks, who would have dispersed the stock and disguised the share ownership, with hundreds of institutional investors pitching in. Once again Morgan's strength was a function of the immature state of the capital markets, which forced him to exercise all his brilliance and ingenuity to locate receptive pockets of capital.

During the protracted industrial depression that began in 1893, J. P. Morgan perfected his mastery of the railroads. As noted earlier, staggering under weighty debt loads and debilitated by internecine competition, many roads went bankrupt and had to be "remorganized" by the Morgan bank. As one-third of the railway system, a gigantic piece of American industry, fell into his lap, Pierpont might have seemed at the zenith of his power, yet greater conquests loomed ahead with the formation of new industrial trusts. To understand the control that Morgan acquired over smokestack America, one must recognize the weak and primitive state of the American banking system west of the Hudson River. As a young, agricultural, debt-ridden nation, the United States had long harbored a deep distrust of bankers. As apostles of the gold standard and hard currency, bankers were associated with eastern elites, foreign financial centers, the absolutist powers of Europe, and extreme inequalities of wealth, and they were regularly blamed for deflation and economic slumps. To curb banker power, the country had killed off the second Bank of the United States in 1832 and opted for a decentralized financial system. Banks weren't allowed to open branches outside their home states and often couldn't even open branches within them. In consequence, the United States had a chaotic system with thousands of small, thinly capitalized community banks, and no large regional or national banks that reflected the emerging size and power of the whole economy, as was the case in Europe.

This stunted, truncated system posed no handicap for American companies until the industrial boom that followed the Civil War. As businesses merged into larger units to compete in national markets and take advantage of economies of scale, their capital needs greatly outstripped the resources of local banks—as we saw with John D. Rockefeller, Sr., and Standard Oil. So the trend toward creating national trusts, which gained momentum in the 1880s and 1890s, pushed small-town businessmen to Wall Street for financing. Had strong regional banks existed as alternatives, there might never have been a J. Pierpont Morgan. The American urge to curb banker power by keeping banks small and poorly capitalized guaranteed, ironically, the dominion of Wall Street, which alone had access to sufficient foreign and domestic capital to form the mammoth trusts.

In 1901, Pierpont Morgan orchestrated the creation of U.S. Steel, a giant integrated steel trust that would dominate every aspect of the business from mining ore to marketing finished products. Capitalized at $1.4 billion—at a time when the capitalization of all American manufacturing came to just $9 billion—it elevated both Wall Street and American industry to a new plateau. To dispose of this small mountain of securities took a monster syndicate of 300 underwriters, including many rich individuals. Many moguls who had brought their companies into U.S. Steel were crude, rough characters who couldn't have negotiated directly with each other and gladly employed the good offices of Pierpont Morgan, who could act as honest broker while summoning forth the necessary capital. Since Morgan already acted as banker to several parties involved in the transaction, he found it easier to win their confidence.

Once again, Morgan was terrifyingly persuasive in coaxing recalcitrant companies to fall into line. At one point, John W. "Bet-a-Million" Gates tried to shake down the negotiators for a higher price for his American Steel and Wire. Suddenly, Morgan, spluttering, furious, appeared in the room, thumped the table emphatically, and roared, "Gentlemen, I am going to leave this building in ten minutes. If by that time you have not accepted our offer, the matter will be closed. We will build our own wire plant." The bluff (if it was one) paid off: Gates capitulated, and Morgan went home, tickled pink by his triumph.

Many small investors were exhilarated by U.S. Steel, which touched off a fever for industrial issues on Wall Street. Many other Americans, however, feared the grim, faceless gigantism of these new leviathans. They worried about the power being usurped by these industrial overlords and what seemed a new greed and materialism corrupting the land. Never a believer in small-scale competition, Morgan was the most visible champion of this new industrial order, though not the most vocal; he never voiced a theory about the trusts or their place in the economy. As with everything, he acted upon principles that seemed luminously clear to him but that he never bothered to articulate or clarify for the public. The old Wall Street felt under no obligation to explain itself either to small investors or the citizenry at large, who then played a negligible role in the world of high finance.

Right after launching U.S. Steel, Pierpont Morgan found himself in a battle royal on the New York Stock Exchange that says much about the Wall Street hierarchy in those days. Morgan was the chief financier for James J. Hill, who had consolidated the Great Northern and Northern Pacific into the major railroad system of the Pacific Northwest. Faithful to Hill, Morgan had thwarted another great railroad magnate, Edward H. Harriman, whom he snobbishly patronized as a two-bit stock-market speculator. Harriman forged a link with Morgan's foremost Wall Street rival, Jacob Schiff of Kuhn, Loeb. After failing to arrive at a truce with Hill, Harriman, aided by Schiff, embarked on one of his most audacious adventures: he secretly began to buy up $78 million in Northern Pacific shares, the largest such operation in stock-market history at that point. If he couldn't strike a deal with Hill, Harriman decided to buy him out. It was a pivotal moment in financial history as the stock market, instead of the banker's study, became the setting for a secret takeover.

At that time, corporate raiders operated under no legal obligation to reveal the size of their stake once a certain threshold had been reached. So while Morgan sunned in the south of France, leaving his partners in charge, Harriman steadily accumulated stock. It took several weeks for the napping Morgan partners to realize that a massive raid against the Northern Pacific was under way. By then, Harriman and Schiff, only 40,000 shares shy of control, had nearly completed their foray. Once apprised of what was happening, Morgan gave orders to buy up the remaining shares at any price. Many short-sellers had already sold borrowed shares of stock, hoping to buy them back at a cheaper price, and as they suddenly rushed to cover their positions, a dangerous scarcity of Northern Pacific stock developed.

Morgan was now hell-bent upon retaining control of the road at any price. After having traded below 100, the stock began to leap upward, jumping hundreds of points between trades, until it reached 1,000; then it dropped a breathtaking 400 points on a single trade. The wild trading in this one stock mesmerized and convulsed the entire exchange, threatening to ruin many speculators.

Calling an armistice in his war with Harriman, Morgan organized a new railroad holding company, the Northern Securities Company, in which both Hill and Harriman were to be represented. For the modern observer, what stands out about the Northern Pacific Corner was how remote Morgan and his partners were from the floor of the New York Stock Exchange. At the time, the top-drawer Street houses, notably J. P. Morgan & Company and Kuhn, Loeb, allocated stocks and bonds through an underwriting syndicate, but neither sold nor traded securities. As someone who considered the market unseemly, J. P. Morgan kept a haughty, fastidious distance from the trading floor. He would no more have appeared at the stock exchange than in a cheap brothel or smoky opium den. In fact, during the 1907 Panic, when Morgan mounted an emergency loan for the stock exchange, he had to ask what time it closed.

After William McKinley was assassinated in September 1901 and Teddy Roosevelt became president, many in the business community worried that the Rough Rider wouldn't perpetuate the probusiness policies of his predecessor, having already upset business interests as a New York assemblyman and governor by referring to Jay Gould and his associates as the "wealthy criminal class" and trying to impose a tax on corporate franchises. When Roosevelt became McKinley's vice president, Wall Street was relieved to be rid of him. Having just launched U.S. Steel and meditating other consolidations—all predicated on a permissive antitrust policy and a laissez-faire president—Morgan was especially apprehensive about the young president. For a short while, Roosevelt, on his best behavior, kept everyone guessing. Then, in February 1902, he revealed his true colors by unexpectedly announcing an antitrust suit against the Northern Securities Company, the railroad holding company that Morgan had formed for his rapprochement between Edward H. Harriman and James J. Hill.

Morgan, learning the bad news at a dinner party, felt deeply betrayed by this ungentlemanly behavior—he thought he should have been consulted—and rushed down to Washington to plead with the president. "If we have done anything wrong," he entreated Roosevelt, "send your man to my man and they can fix it up." Roosevelt's "man" was Attorney General Philander C. Knox, while Morgan's "man" was his personal attorney. Cynically amused, Roosevelt realized that Morgan was treating him less as a U.S. president than as a fellow mogul. He commented afterward, "This is a most illuminating illustration of the Wall Street point of view. Mr. Morgan could not help regarding me as a big rival operator, who either intended to ruin all his interests or else could be induced to come to an agreement to ruin none." At this apogee of banker power, it seemed perfectly natural that a Wall Street tycoon could hurry down to the White House and barge in on the president.

For a trust-busting president like Roosevelt, Morgan was a wonderful foil for establishing his reformist credentials. With his watch-chain drawn across his pear-shaped silhouette, his top hat and lethal cigars, Morgan was a cartoon plutocrat come to life, the very embodiment of Wall Street. (In the 1880s, one medical sage had advised him to give up exercise to preserve his health; to such advice we perhaps owe the sleek contours of the turn-of-the-century tycoon.) For Roosevelt, Morgan was always a handy symbol to manipulate. When T.R. issued his famous denunciation of "malefactors of great wealth" at the Gridiron Club in 1907, some reporters thought his gaze conspicuously traveled toward Morgan in the audience.

Yet one can make the case that Morgan and Roosevelt were blood brothers under the skin. Both men of irrepressible vitality, veteran travelers with a romantic sense of history, they were the two most powerful personalities of their era. Morgan was a flashing, roaring engine of a man with eyes so piercing that one observer famously likened them to the headlights of an oncoming locomotive. When he sat for the photographer Edward Steichen, he seized one arm of the chair so violently that it looked like he was grasping a knife. Roosevelt, with his glinting spectacles, big grin, and vigorous step, was no less vivid a presence. One British statesman who visited America said that he had witnessed two great wonders of nature—Niagara Falls and President Roosevelt. Another observer said Roosevelt's personality was so strong that you had to wring him from your clothes afterward.

Both Morgan and Roosevelt came from well-to-do families that could trace their American ancestry back to the seventeenth century. Since they had been cofounders of the American Museum of Natural History, Morgan had actually known Roosevelt's father. While many in their social circle condemned the new industrialism as a threat to the old patrician order, both Morgan and Roosevelt were robust, forward-looking men and devout believers in change, for all their reverence for the past and aristocratic credentials.

Far from favoring a return to the nineteenth-century economy of small-scale entrepreneurs, Roosevelt saw the new trusts as a natural outgrowth of ineluctable economic trends. You could no more stop the trusts, he said, than you could dam the Mississippi River—a position that would distinguish him from such progressive figures as Woodrow Wilson, who wanted to break up the trusts. Roosevelt wanted to use government regulation to root out bad, abusive trusts so that good trusts could flourish unhampered by bothersome socialist reformers. For all the rhetorical shadowboxing between Morgan and Roosevelt, they probably worked together much more often than they sparred. U.S. Steel and other trusts created under the Morgan aegis generally cooperated with the antitrust investigations of Roosevelt's new Bureau of Corporations and fared better than many of their counterparts. In contrast, Standard Oil never conceded the legitimacy of government

supervision of the economy and because of its hard-line, obstruc-
tionist tactics, ended up bearing the full brunt of the Roosevelt-
Taft antitrust policy.

By birthright and nature, J. P. Morgan was a solid establishmentarian, a stalwart believer in order and hierarchy in all things,
whether financial, religious, or governmental. He wasn't unalter-
ably opposed to government involvement in economic life, which
isn't surprising: much of his financial success came from collabo-
rating with the U.S. government, including refunding Civil War
debt in the 1870s. In 1895, acting in concert with the London Rothschilds, Morgan aided President Grover Cleveland in rescuing the
gold standard, raising $65 million and stemming the flow of gold
from U.S. government vaults. For Victorian merchant bankers,
governments ranked among their major clients and so when it
came to regulation, they couldn't very well turn around and dis-
pute the legitimacy of all government action. What Morgan did
object to vigorously was being subjected to public interrogation,
as if he were a scoundrel instead of a great patriot—a pained attitude clearly evident during the 1912 Pujo hearings.

The mutual ambivalence of the Morgan–Roosevelt relationship was in evidence during the anthracite coal strike of 1902.
When the mine owners reacted to the strike with medieval feroc-
ity, Roosevelt didn't send in the militia but opted for a more en-
lightened approach: arbitration. With the mines owned by
railroads under Morgan's thumb, Roosevelt enlisted his coopera-
tion to coax the owners into a peaceful settlement of the strike. In
this heyday of banker power, the Wall Street financier was the political emissary of his client. In the end, Roosevelt wrote an effu-
sive tribute to Morgan: "If it had not been for your going in the
matter, I do not see how the strike could have been settled at this
time, and the consequences that might have followed are very
dreadful to contemplate."

The essential affinity between Morgan and Roosevelt was

perhaps best exhibited during the 1907 Panic. Once again, the popular view of the banker as traitorous bogeyman had left the country bereft of a central bank or lender of last resort. Pierpont Morgan stepped into the breach as the ersatz central banker, once again capitalizing, paradoxically, on national hostility toward bankers. As trust companies toppled in October 1907, touching off runs on many sound banks, Morgan rushed back from an Episcopal Convention in Richmond and, like a commanding general, took charge of his troops. Caught sleeping by events, Roosevelt sent Treasury Secretary George B. Cortelyou to New York. Instead of presiding over a federal rescue operation, Cortelyou put $25 million in government funds at Morgan's disposal. In the following days, acting like a one-man Federal Reserve system, Morgan decided which firms would fail and which survive. Through a nonstop flurry of meetings, he organized rescues of banks and trust companies, averted a shutdown of the New York Stock Exchange, and engineered a financial bailout of New York City. In a crisis Morgan was unsurpassed because he wasn't troubled by the doubts that seemed to paralyze mere mortals. He believed in certain verities and acted with the force of an invincible simplicity. Had he been more cerebral or more complicated, he might not have been half so effective. The 1907 Panic was his finest hour— what T.R. might have termed his "crowded hour" of glory.

Morgan had a flair for handling crises, a thespian's sense of timing and backdrop, which he employed to great effect. To prod reluctant trust company presidents to contribute to a $25-million rescue fund, he invited them to his ornate library one evening, where they deliberated beneath the sorrowing gaze of madonnas, saints, and other Renaissance masterpieces staring down from the walls. In a brilliant coup de théâtre, he announced that he had locked the great bronze doors of the library and wouldn't let anybody leave until they had come to terms. Meanwhile, Morgan coolly played solitaire in an adjoining room, periodically rejecting proposals presented to him. At a quarter to five in the morning, Morgan shoved a pen and paper into the hands of Edward King, leader of the trust presidents, and said firmly, "Here's the place, King. And here's the pen." Once the papers were signed, the doors were opened and the bankers emerged wanly into the early-morning air. The 1907 Panic persuaded many skeptics that the country needed a central bank and couldn't rely upon the theatrics of aging tycoons any longer. As Senator Nelson Aldrich said, "Something has got to be done. We may not always have Pierpont Morgan with us to meet a banking crisis." Morgan's role helped to spur passage of the Federal Reserve Act in 1913. As a strong adherent of a central bank—albeit one, like the Bank of England, controlled by private bankers—Morgan contributed his chief partner, Henry P. Davison, as an adviser to Senator Aldrich on the matter.

Throughout his career, J. Pierpont Morgan possessed more power than money, although he had a great deal of both. The key to understanding his influence was that he represented the masses of investors who delegated authority to him and worshipfully followed his lead. As the uncontested master of manipulating other people's money, he took the latent power of domestic and overseas investors and converted it into an active managerial role, blurring the line between industry and commerce. Pierpont Morgan was the intermediary par excellence and he had the good fortune to live at a moment when the middleman loomed larger in the financial equation than at any other time in Anglo-American financial history.

TYCOONS II:

The Warburgs

In the historic evolution of the banker, the saga of the Warburg family takes us back to that dim, indistinct dawn when commerce imperceptibly metamorphosed into finance. It spotlights the transitional moment when the pawnbroker or moneylender or even dealer in secondhand clothing began to shade over into the figure we call the banker. As we saw with Mayer Amschel Rothschild, this mutation was gradual and almost unnoticed, with banking slowly emerging from a blend of businesses to assert its preeminent importance. The Rothschild patriarch probably didn't think of himself as a "banker," which would have seemed too restrictive a self-definition for so versatile a figure.

A good deal of poppycock has been spoken, often among Jews themselves, about supposed Jewish cleverness with money, but the phenomenon of the Jewish banker arose from other sources. In medieval and Renaissance Europe, Jews labored humbly in those interstices of the economy shunned by Christians. In a world ruled by prohibitions, they couldn't, in many places, belong to guilds, farm land, or trade in many products and so entered banking by default. At the time, the Church construed the Bible to mean that Christians were proscribed from lending money at interest. A special stratum of Jews was therefore plucked from obscurity and established—at the express wish of the Christian community—as a privileged banking caste. As creatures of politics, not markets, elevated by prejudice, not preference, the Jewish bankers occupied a precarious perch. We must remember that they performed economically necessary activities then considered taboo by Christians. Their royal patrons must have felt vaguely guilty about employing their services, for how could one entirely respect people who conducted activities that—if done by Christians—would have been deemed sinful? In the subconscious of the gentile community, the taint of uncleanliness must have clung to the image of the Jewish banker.

The need for ready credit was pressing in both the political and the economic spheres, for many noblemen had pretensions that far exceeded the scant resources at their disposal. In an age lacking strong exchequers or central banks, how were petty rulers to outfit armies with horses and guns, build ornate palaces and strong fortifications, splendid parks and gardens, and prosecute foreign military adventures? How were they to adorn their persons, decorate their carriages, and spread out sumptuous banquet tables? France could draw upon a powerful central bureaucracy and Italy a highly developed banking system, but the 250 duchies, principalities, kingdoms, and city-states strewn across German-speaking central Europe suffered under special handicaps. They needed moneylenders expert at foreign exchange who could create a unified trading zone amid a hodgepodge of monies and restrictive customs regulations. In particular, the long, gruelling Thirty Years' War (1618–48) depleted the treasuries of many princes, threatening their status in the Holy Roman Empire.

Into this spacious gap between noble aspirations and empty coffers stepped the *Hofjuden*, or Court Jews, who advised monarchs, arranged loans, and performed diverse financial services, frequently under the appellation of court "factor" or agent. It was much easier for the sovereign to borrow from Jewish bankers than to levy unpopular taxes. As creatures of the Diaspora, with tightly knit family networks extended across several states, Jews were strategically placed to handle cross-border transactions. In exchange for their services, they attained not only wealth and power, but a social standing that would have been a daydream for other Jews. Some Jewish bankers accumulated titles as a reward for their financial dexterity and services to the crown.

In the late nineteenth century, under the twin impulses of empire and emancipation, the German Jews as a group would advance into the middle class and populate the professions. In earlier centuries, however, Jewish bankers were conspicuous exceptions in their ragged, impoverished communities. What an abyss yawned between them and their less-fortunate brethren, and what fears they must have harbored of being stripped of their privileges and of tumbling back into the masses. Indeed, many of the Court Jews slipped back into their former lowly status after two or three generations. Bequeathed such a perilous eminence, the Court Jew had to be both proud and officious, assertive and cautious—in brief, a walking contradiction.

It took a delicate balancing act, a certain mental toughness, to travel in two such contrasting worlds: that of the rarefied court, where the Jew's place was inevitably uncertain, and that of the gloomy ghetto, where his place was unfortunately all too well assured. No matter how rich, every Court Jew had known abuse from some sadistic aristocrat or minor functionary and often incurred the displeasure of courtiers who profited from corrupt, inefficient treasuries. As did Mayer Amschel Rothschild, Court Jews needed to thank their patrons fervently, to shower them with gifts and servile flattery, to crook the knee regularly. Having Jewish bankers at their mercy, rulers were tempted to behave in an arbitrary, high-handed fashion, reneging on agreements, or, if it suited their convenience, repudiating loans outright. Other than silently bewailing their fate, Jewish bankers had no recourse in combating such injustice—part of their irresistible attraction for sovereigns. And if they ever thought to protest such injustice, the periodic pogroms and attacks against them reminded them of their vulnerability. For all their grandeur, the Court Jews suffered the enmity that attached to Jews and bankers both.

The schizoid life of the Court Jews—religious and secular, Jewish and assimilated—must have been disorienting. While supplicants at court, they reigned as veritable deities in the Jewish community, where they were expected to care for community organizations and succor their poor. They were, at once, extremely remote from and intimately involved with other Jews. Even Court Jews who ceased to have dealings with other Jews never entirely lost an uneasy sense of their distant ghetto roots.

The Warburgs were never quite fancy enough to count as Court Jews and occupied a less-exalted rung on the gilded ladder—that of *Schutzjuden,* or "protected Jews." In 1559, the Prince-Bishop of Paderborn imported Simon von Cassel into the Westphalian town of Warburg, granting him a *Schutzvertrag,* or protective charter, that enabled him to work as a moneychanger and pawnbroker, and ensuring religious tolerance for him and his family. Simon made a decent living, as evidenced by his large timbered residence, which still stands today. Despite the advantages that accompanied his charter, Simon had to put up with punitive tax rates that surpassed those imposed on Christian residents—a gentle hint that, however superior to other Jews, he remained distinctly subordinate to the Christian community. He served as emissary between two worlds, interpreting the prince to the Jewish community, while serving as advocate for his poor brethren in any altercations with Christian authorities. While all merchant bankers cultivated the good graces of royal courts to drum up business, Jewish bankers needed the state's sanction simply to exist. Whatever indignities they suffered, they developed an exaggerated and sometimes obsequious regard for the authorities who allowed them to practice business.

In the late seventeenth century, Simon's descendants moved to Altona, situated on the Elbe River in northern Germany, then relocated in 1773 to the neighboring city-state of Hamburg. (Since German Jews couldn't take surnames, they frequently adopted their home-town names; by this point, the family had dropped the "von Cassel," retaining the name of their former Westphalian town, Warburg.) In 1798, the Warburgs started M.M. Warburg & Company, destined to become Germany's most prestigious private bank by the Nazi era. To give some perspective on the Warburgs' ancient lineage, by 1798 they had already been in the banking business for two and a half centuries; by contrast, Mayer Amschel Rothschild that year was a twenty-five-year-old peddler of rare coins who was hoping to strike up some promising relations with wealthy clients.

While the Warburgs started out under the shelter of a Christian sovereign, they escaped the entire system of *Hofjuden* and *Schutzjuden* when they migrated north. Altona existed under the benign rule of the Danes, who extended ample liberties to Jews. So, by the late eighteenth century, the Warburgs had journeyed far from their former oppressive world of forelock-tugging and royal condescension and inhabited something closer to the modern world. In the Frankfurt of the young Mayer Amschel Rothschild, Jews were still immured in the ghetto and destined to live out their lives along the dank, shadowy Judengasse. They could venture into the Christian city only on business, couldn't stroll two abreast, and couldn't linger in a park or café for refreshment. So fearful were Christians of contamination that the windows of Jewish homes facing the Christian community were boarded up, lest Jewish eyes should defile Gentile pedestrians.

In comparison, Hamburg seemed a paradise of tolerance. It

hadn't by any means banished all anti-Semitic restrictions: Jews could rent but not own their residences and were confined to certain streets. Yet, unlike the barbarous treatment of Frankfurt Jews, the Hamburg Jews enjoyed many benefits of citizenship. What made Hamburg so peculiarly receptive to the Jewish community? The town had the tolerant, open-minded spirit that has blown through so many ports, entrepôts, and other commercial crossroads throughout history. A former member of the Hanseatic League, near the North Sea and the Baltic Sea, it formed part of a broad, international trading culture, and was tied by vital commercial links to Russia, Scandinavia, Holland, England, and other maritime nations; it was therefore less susceptible to the bigotry that has historically flourished in rural, backward places less exposed to other cultures.

The Hamburg Jews also profited from a democratic civic culture that was reflected in the town's elected councils and other public institutions, things not found in the little inland kingdoms and principalities. Capitalism invigorated the North German ports long before its rationalizing, material values penetrated interior regions. Hamburg's leading citizens weren't feckless aristocrats but prosperous burghers who tended to value money and enterprise above noble birth. There was snobbery galore, to be sure, but it revolved around money, not titles. The old Hamburg merchant families would have appreciated Voltaire's portrait of the meritocracy he encountered on the London Stock Exchange in the early 1730s: "Go into the London Exchange, a place more dignified than many a royal court. There you will find representatives of every nation quietly assembled to promote human welfare. There the Jew, the Mahometan, and the Christian deal with each other as though they were all of the same religion. They call no man Infidel unless he be bankrupt."

In the early nineteenth century, the Warburgs were still a provincial banking power, yet such middling success spared them

the pomp and pomposity, not to mention the assimilation, that be-
set the Jewish grandees. They had enough success to be confident,
but also enough failure to be skeptical, even fatalistic, about their
place in the world. (As the first Siegmund Warburg said in the
nineteenth century, "It has been the Warburgs' good fortune that
whenever we were about to get very rich, something happened to
make us poor and we had to start all over again.") Like many
other Jewish bankers, they acted as local agents for the Rothschilds and cultivated them no less assiduously than the Rothschilds did the Christian nobility. As a mark of this extreme
deference, the Warburgs stocked special stationery for letters to
the Rothschilds, and even hired a man gifted with magnificent
penmanship to scribe letters to them. The Warburgs' rise to power
proceeded in tandem with the emergence of heavy industry and
the growth of the German state, while the Rothschilds owed their
initial success to royal patronage; in that sense, the Rothschilds
represented an earlier stage in financial history. When the Warburgs helped to quell a financial panic in Hamburg in 1857 by ar-
ranging for a temporary shipment of silver ingots from Vienna,
they acted on behalf of the Hamburg Senate, not some local
despot, reflecting the rising influence of the financial middleman.

*T*he fortunes of the Warburgs surged ahead spectacularly during the era of the Famous Five brothers—Aby, Max, Paul, Felix,
and Fritz—all born between 1866 and 1879. The dates are worth
noting because they overlap with the two great formative experi-
ences of the German Jews: emancipation—the removal of the last
legal impediments against them—and the forging of the German
Empire under Bismarck. This confluence of events was extremely
significant, for the semiconscious equation of emancipation and
empire spawned the stereotypical, supernationalistic German
Jew. As much as any family, the Warburgs responded to the new

opportunities with boundless gusto and self-confidence; they would exhibit, in bold relief, the élan of a Jewish community newly liberated from the weighty shackles of past centuries. At the same time, they remained poised on the knife edge of the German–Jewish contradiction, afraid of leaning too far toward or away from their Jewish roots. They wished to be German and Jewish at the same time and in equal measure, and for a long time the two traditions, the two identities, seemed to be more symbiotic than incompatible.

The five brothers present a fascinating spectrum of personalities, since each seems to reflect a different compromise with the contradictory status of the German Jew. As the eldest son of a Jewish banking dynasty, Aby Warburg should rightfully have been the senior partner of M.M. Warburg & Company, but this bookish young man found banking dull. At age thirteen, he struck a very biblical-sounding deal with the second brother, Max, age twelve, by selling him his birthright. Max could become the bank's senior partner, Aby proposed, if he submitted to a simple agreement: he would buy Aby, in exchange, all the books he wanted for the rest of his life. Later, Max joked ruefully that had he known he was handing over a blank check to one of the century's most compulsive bibliophiles, he might have thought twice about the wisdom of the bargain. In the end, Aby went on a lifelong book-buying spree, acquiring 80,000 books, many of them rare and costly, not to speak of thousands of slides and photos.

As an art history student, Aby began to envision a unique interdisciplinary library, one that would track the theoretical associations and imaginative leaps of his mind rather than the standard, plodding subject arrangement. There were two trends in late-nineteenth-century libraries that he deplored: the proliferation of specialized libraries, which forced a wide-ranging scholar to forrage among separate collections if he wished to study the philosophy, psychology, art history, poetry, politics, and religion of a given period; and the disappearance of open stacks, which precluded the welcome discoveries and startling, synthetic links that accompany idle browsing of library shelves. Aby was determined to create a library that would restore the freewheeling adventure inherent in the old library experience. By the early 1900s this bibliomaniac was purchasing about 500 books per year, which created storage problems and forced him to occupy a new home in 1909. Soon, like some metastasizing science-fiction monster, the books were heaped in every cranny of the house, including the lavatory. Shelves creaked, floors warped, walls groaned: his brothers feared for the house's structural safety and decided to build Aby a separate library next door.

Aby Warburg was a voluble, hyperkinetic man, a brilliant little windbag, who seemed to have absorbed, like a sponge, all of Western civilization, and he gladly regurgitated his learning to any listener for hours on end. As a private scholar and the offspring of a rich family, he never had to earn money and importunately dunned his brothers (who were alternately mesmerized and exasperated by his persistent entreaties) for more money for his library. Whenever his brothers resisted, Aby would say that other rich families had their racing stables, and the Warburgs would have their library. He prophesied that his library would outlive their banks—which very nearly came true in the 1930s. While it may seem strange that a banking family should have humored such a son, it formed part of an honorable Jewish tradition of supporting a son who was a rabbi or talmudic scholar, thus bringing honor to the family and enriching the community. As a product of the Court Jew tradition, the Jewish banker was expected to be a patron of the arts and letters.

While a superb mimic and veteran prankster, Aby periodically yielded to fathomless gloom, and as he moved into middle age his psychiatric problems only worsened. A fanatical nationalist, he was convinced that German culture was far superior to the lowly shopkeeping mentality that governed the Anglo-Saxon world. He believed this so strongly that Germany's defeat in the Great War triggered a mental breakdown. As an art history scholar in a world permeated by anti-Semitism, Aby had often been stung by prejudice, even though he had rigidly, sometimes testily, distanced himself from his family's religious heritage. In the delirious ravings that accompanied his breakdown, he darkly confessed his fear that he was a secret Christian. Always fiercely defiant when faced with anti-Semitism, he succumbed to a Jewish form of self-hatred—a phenomenon common enough among persecuted minorities.

For nearly six years, Aby stayed cooped up in a Swiss asylum, wavering between madness and lucidity, and it seemed improbable that he would ever emerge again. Yet he courageously used his mental illness to gain new insights into the pagan, irrational currents that lay beneath the outward serenity of classical art. In the end, he worked out an agreement with the sanitarium head that, if he could successfully deliver a lecture to the inmates, he could go home. Reaching back into his past, he gave an extraordinary lecture on the serpent ritual of the Pueblo Indians of New Mexico, whom he had visited as a young man back in the 1890s. On the strength of this, he emerged from the asylum in 1924, the same year, coincidentally, that Thomas Mann published *The Magic Mountain*.

When Aby returned to his private library in Hamburg, it had been transformed in his absence into a public institution, affiliated with the University of Hamburg. Prized as a cultural ornament of Weimar Germany for its outstanding lectures, seminars, and publications, it attracted such eminent scholars as Ernst Cassirer and Erwin Panofsky. For five years, before he died in 1929, Aby enjoyed the new renown of his library. His library outlived him, but not exactly as he had pictured it. In the spring of 1933, when the Nazis began to make monitory pyres of forbidden books, the Warburgs naturally feared that they would incinerate Aby's books. In late 1933, they hurriedly packed the books into 531 boxes, loaded them on two small ships, and sent the library to London disguised as a "temporary loan," which, luckily, became a permanent one. Today the Warburg Institute stands on Woburn Square in Bloomsbury and forms part of the University of London.

Of the five brothers it was Max who felt the full exhilaration of empire and emancipation, giving him a robust energy, an unflagging optimism. He had shed the deep-seated inhibitions that had constrained his ancestors and believed, in a glandular way, that Germany was a place of infinite hope for Jews. As a young man, Max joined a Bavarian cavalry regiment, and, notwithstanding his boyhood pact with Aby, flirted with a career as a military officer. Such a notion would have seemed outlandish to Jews of an earlier day and was still scarcely conceivable to older Jews who knew that anti-Semitism was rampant in the officer corps. Understandably edgy about parental approval, Max sat down and, in a rather defensive spirit, composed a sixteen-page letter to his father, Moritz, outlining his plans to become an officer. After an excruciating delay, he received a letter of surpassing eloquence from his father, which read in its entirety: "My dear Max, meschugge [crazy]. Your loving father."

Dragooned back to the family bank in Hamburg, Max took up his foreordained place in the dynasty's history. He was not only a sanguine young man but almost totally fearless, devoid of the self-protective caution that had long been indispensable for Jewish survival. In 1892, when Max was twenty-five, a severe cholera epidemic struck Hamburg, killing up to a thousand people a day; in the end, 8,000 victims died. As people fled the streets, and even stopped shaking hands with each other, Max strode resolutely through this grim landscape of death as if endowed with a charmed life. From seven in the morning until midnight, he manned his station on the ground floor of the bank as carts, piled high with coffins, trundled by his window. As he later remarked, "I had the certain feeling that I was immune." This spirit, optimism, and faith in the future were emblematic of Jews in Imperial Germany.

Later on, in the overheated fantasies of Nazi pamphleteers, Jewish bankers were portrayed as members of a global conspiracy, plotting Germany's ruin. As the career of Max Warburg shows, this libel exactly inverted the truth, for Jewish bankers served the German state to a fault. Since they weren't answerable to shareholders and had no need to disclose information to the investing public, the small private banking houses were perfect back channels for confidential diplomatic missions. At a time when Kaiser Wilhelm II declared that Germany's future lay at sea, M.M. Warburg joined the consortium that financed the Hamburg–American Line, the world's foremost shipping concern at the end of the nineteenth century. Much in the manner of Pierpont Morgan with the railroads, Max Warburg went on the board of the shipping line, forging links between finance and commerce that would increasingly characterize the concentrated German economy.

In his foreign investments, Max followed the meticulous guidance of the Foreign Office. In 1910 he created the Hamburg Morocco Society with the dual purpose of promoting German mining in northwest Africa and throwing down the gauntlet to French power in the region. After the First World War, Max served on the German financial delegation at Versailles, where he indignantly protested the level of reparations. Since they financed global trade and straddled the overseas flow of capital, the old-line private bankers had the financial expertise and international vision to carry on such talks. For his troubles, Max was falsely blamed by the Nazis for having sold out Germany to the Allies.

With five ambitious sons to marry off, the Warburgs had ample opportunity for dynastic matches, which were needed to preserve and extend the banking capital of their private partnership. Paul and Felix, the third and fourth sons, respectively, proved to be highly adept in this department. In 1895, Felix married Frieda Schiff, the daughter of Jacob Schiff, managing partner of the investment house of Kuhn, Loeb and second only to Pierpont Morgan among Wall Street's Olympians. That same year, Paul married Nina Loeb, the daughter of Solomon Loeb, the founder of Kuhn, Loeb. These marriages gave the Warburgs unmatched access to Wall Street capital and, at first glance, look much less like romantic flings than well-timed business moves. Surely two sons - couldn't, by chance, have stumbled into such choice marriages. Yet the more one studies the preliminaries of these marriages, the more one is forced to conclude—in the face of all logic and probability—that they reflected genuine passion, not cool business calculation. The Warburgs were a lucky family: the promptings of the heart always led them straight to windfall profits.

After seven years with Max at M.M. Warburg, Paul yielded to the homesick Nina and they moved to New York, where he took up a partnership at Kuhn, Loeb. In a family bubbling with high spirits and quick-witted repartee, Paul was shy and professorial, often bowed beneath melancholy. An incorruptible man with an exceptionally keen mind for economics, he was that rare financier who wished to apply his intelligence to the public weal instead of to his bank account. Soon after he arrived, Wall Street had another of its familiar, recurring panics, again exposing the costly absence of a central bank in America. Well-versed in European finance, Paul extemporaneously drafted an essay on the need for an American central bank, then realized that it would be a shade presumptuous to lecture the natives after such short residence in New York; so he buried the essay in his drawer. Only after the 1907 Panic did he dust it off and publish it in *The New York Times*. As a result, he soon found himself drawn into the turbulent crusade to create the Federal Reserve System, which would prove a triumph on a personal no less than a political level. Morbidly shy, almost phobic about public speaking, he also suffered from having a foreign accent and still being a German citizen. (Only in 1911 did he become an American citizen.) Most scholars credit him with being a principal—perhaps the principal—architect of the Federal Reserve. Woodrow Wilson crowned his effort by appointing him to the first Federal Reserve Board in 1914 and naming him the first vice chairman in 1916.

We shall look at Paul's wartime experience in Washington in a moment, but, before doing so, we should note his stellar financial clairvoyance. In March 1929, he predicted the Wall Street Crash and subsequent Great Depression with matchless clarity when he issued the following unhedged forecast: "If a stock-exchange debauch is quickly arrested by prompt and determined action, it is not too much to hope that a shrinkage of inflated stock prices may be brought about without seriously affecting the wider circle of general business. If orgies of unrestrained speculation are permitted to spread too far, however, the ultimate collapse is certain not only to affect the speculators themselves, but also to bring about a general depression involving the entire country." More than most prophets, financial prophets are doomed to be derided or ignored—too much money is being bet the other way—and the accuracy of Paul's warning was quickly confirmed by the uniformly hostile reception it received.

In a family loaded with central European angst, Felix, son number four, displayed a sunny vivacity and zest that left the rest of the family exhausted from his ceaseless activities. His nickname, "Fizzie," paid homage to his effervescent personality. That he seemed proof against depression, a stranger to the blues, was acknowledged by friends who alluded to bright, cloudless days as "Felix weather." Never a ponderous theoretician, Felix nevertheless had a delightful wit and left behind a trail of aphorisms. He would lecture his family that "children should be obscene but not absurd," and once gave his friend Albert Einstein his own version of relativity: "Everything is relative except for relatives and they, alas, are constant." This truth applied with special force to the contentious Warburg clan.

Though a lifelong Kuhn, Loeb partner, Felix never displayed any particular talent for banking. Finance for him was a form of black magic he never mastered. Once, his youngest son, Edward, was leaving on a trip and came to him for money. Felix gave him a thick wad of traveler's cheques but unfortunately countersigned them in advance, later leaving his poor son stranded out West without money. (So much for myths about Jewish cleverness with money.) Humanity was better served that he devoted his Kuhn, Loeb tenure to philanthropy. A one-man conglomerate of good causes, he was a founder or seminal figure in almost all the major Jewish charities that arose early in the century, including the American Jewish Committee, the Joint Distribution Committee, and the Federation of Jewish Philanthropies. Among immigrant masses packed into the tenements of the Lower East Side of Manhattan, Felix Warburg was a mythical benefactor, his name attached to many settlement houses, playgrounds, and summer camps.

Nowadays it seems odd that Felix was able to spend most of his time at Kuhn, Loeb managing philanthropic commitments, or that Jacob Schiff allowed Paul to be seconded to Washington. Why did the firm tolerate this? It was partly vestigial, perpetuating the Court Jew tradition by which the Jewish banker served as a community elder, assuming a wide range of charitable obligations. And at a time when wholesale banks counted governments among their most important clients, Paul's government work promised collateral benefits for Kuhn, Loeb in the form of government contacts or superior knowledge of financial conditions. Felix's pro bono work also says much about the leisurely Wall Street life in the days of relationship banking. The hours tended to be short, the demands few. For the most illustrious houses, investment banking was a matter of holding on to the existing clientele and making the clientele feel pampered; Felix Warburg's social skills must have helped in that cause. The pro bono tradition had other decided benefits. Partners who were prominent in civic and philanthropic affairs brought in clients, such as universities, churches, hospitals, synagogues, and other institutions, with large endowments to manage.

Rounding out our survey of the Famous Five brothers, we should mention the youngest, Fritz, the only one, strictly speaking, who was not famous. He was a torpid, shambling man with a warm, earthy personality and an enormous walrus moustache. This homely man was probably the most humane of the five brothers. Born into a brood of notorious overachievers, he always felt a bit inadequate, since he was neither a genius nor a world-historical figure. If he seems a lesser personage than the others, his résumé was more than respectable. Besides being a junior partner of M.M. Warburg & Company in Hamburg, he chaired the Jewish hospital and Jewish community board in Hamburg and headed the local metals exchange. In 1938 he became the lone Warburg to be imprisoned by the Nazis and was only released months later when the Nazis extorted a large ransom payment from the family.

Before considering the most remarkable Warburg, Sir Siegmund Warburg, it might be worth lingering for a moment on the political troubles that bedeviled the Famous Five. During the First World War, Max Warburg advised the kaiser on German finances, while brother Paul, on the other side of the conflict, advised Woodrow Wilson at the Federal Reserve Board. While Paul couldn't scrub from his psyche every trace of German sympathy, he conscientiously served his adopted country. Yet such was the anti-German hysteria that Woodrow Wilson cravenly refused to renew his appointment for another Fed term in 1918. (In his pri-

vate papers, Paul averred that some political enemies had also settled old scores under the convenient cover of chauvinistic outrage.) It was a terrible disappointment to Paul that he had to
renounce his meager Washington salary and return to Wall Street
to resume a princely income.

Paul Warburg's Washington debacle tells its own instructive
tale about the mythology of the Jewish banker. Starting in the
1920s, Nazi propagandists presented the Warburgs and their kin
as rootless "cosmopolitans" devoid of true national loyalties, their
allegiance pledged to a nefarious global conspiracy committed,
for some inexplicable reason, to Germany's ruin. With extensive
business and family interests in several countries, Jewish bankers
were always vulnerable to such nonsensical hate-mongering. Like
other private bankers in the nineteenth century, they often operated through a cluster of interlocking partnerships in various financial capitals. To further their business connections and fatten
up their capital—as private partnerships, they didn't have access
to the public markets to boost their capital base—they also en-
couraged marriages to other banking families. It was therefore
possible—if malicious and totally absurd—to take the Warburg
family tree, all their lusty wooing and wedding, and interpret it as
a secret blueprint for global financial domination.

Given the global nature of their business, it was only natural
that Jewish bankers were tolerant and internationalist by nature.
They were typically well traveled and multilingual, schooled in
several countries, and at home in many cultures and currencies.
Yet the world never allowed them the luxury of their internation-
alism. During political crises, they had to beat a quick retreat from
their overseas affiliates and even family members and align themselves with their home governments. (During the First World War,
the American and German Warburgs couldn't even correspond
with one another.) In the early days of the First World War, Max
Warburg conducted a fervent, if eventually futile, correspondence

with Jacob Schiff, trying to enlist his financial support for Germany. At first, in a near-suicidal move, Schiff wouldn't allow Kuhn, Loeb to participate in the $500-million Anglo-French loan of 1915, led by J. P. Morgan & Company. Having grown up in Germany and having built much of his career on German financial ties, Schiff found it extremely difficult to execute a sudden, expedient volte-face. In the end, he couldn't resist the pro-Allied fervor on Wall Street and the following year fell into line and began raising money for France. He not only kept Max Warburg at bay, but in blunt, forceful letters to him disclosed his grave doubts about the authoritarian nature of German society.

Just as the Great War dispelled soothing, socialist fantasies that class fidelity would count for more than patriotic ardor in wartime and that proles across Europe would never fight each other, so the war destroyed the notion that "international bankers" operated in a sphere above political strife and could pursue agendas that transcended national ties. No matter that the First World War gave the lie to the image of the "cosmopolitan" Jewish banker: the Nazis, as was their wont, chose to ignore inconvenient facts.

*I*f banking is a dull subject, then God, in His infinite mercy, has provided some compensation for the beleaguered financial historian by creating a few extremely colorful bankers to enliven things. It's hard to imagine that the world of *haute banque* has produced a more extraordinary citizen than Sir Siegmund Warburg, who started his career at M.M. Warburg & Company during the Weimar years. Unlike his Hamburg cousins, he grew up an only child amid the secluded charms of the Swabian Alps in southwest Germany, where he read an enormous amount. Siegmund would always show the quirky erudition and eclectic tastes of the true autodidact. His father—a sickly, troubled man who died in his early fifties—ceded control of Siegmund's upbringing to his cerebral, strong-willed wife, Lucie, who trained her son to be a perfectionist and exacting rationalist. Each night she prayed with the boy at his bedside, imparting the following advice: "When you pray, the most important thing is to think very hard about all the wrong things you have done during the day. And if you cannot think of at least five or six or seven things you have done wrong, then something is wrong with you." It was not exactly a training calculated to produce a light-hearted, well-adjusted little boy.

During the nineteenth century, the control of M.M. Warburg & Company was shared between two branches of the family named after the Hamburg streets they inhabited: the Mittelweg wing, which fielded the Famous Five, and the often envious Alsterufer wing, who had fallen behind their cousins. Siegmund was the up-and-coming star of the embattled Alsterufer clan and he tended to look with great ambivalence upon the self-important strivings and braggadocio of the Mittelweg Warburgs. As head of the Berlin office of M.M. Warburg in the early 1930s, Siegmund concluded that his superior talent would be spurned by his Mittelweg relatives and that nepotism would destroy his chances to win a succession fight. As black sheep of the family and a brilliant loner (despite a wide circle of friends), he seemed uniquely sensitive to the dark, subterranean currents in German society. Perhaps the rationality inculcated in him by his mother endowed him with a heightened awareness of Nazi irrationality. He was also a man who respected revelatory signs—what he always called "hints of fate"—and he saw many of them when Hitler seized power in 1933. With a prescience that seemed almost a family trait, Siegmund saw the terrible shape of things to come and fled to England with his lovely Swedish wife and two children.

Siegmund Warburg provides us with an intriguing historical experiment. What happens when you take a financial dynasty, cut it off at its peak, strip it of its capital, and force it to relocate and start over again? Can the scions of inherited wealth succeed without the advantages of birth they once enjoyed? Could Siegmund Warburg re-create, by dint of brains and drive, his former place in the world? In October 1934, Siegmund, thirty-two, and three other people launched the New Trading Company in London, a tiny outfit that grew, prospered, and was renamed S.G. Warburg & Company in 1946. By the early 1960s this small, decidedly upstart house—it had started out in the shadow of the Rothschilds and Barings, the Morgans and Hambros—was England's premier investment house. It is hard to overstate Siegmund's achievement, for he had pulled off this minor miracle at a time when the City of London was anti-Semitic and anti-German, inbred and xenophobic. There was also an almost visceral hostility to the innovation he represented.

How had he managed this feat? First, he had exhibited a painstaking, almost compulsive, attention to detail, and fondly quoted Uncle Aby, the art historian, who often said that the Good Lord lived in the details. Siegmund thought a firm's stress on excellence should be visible, from the largest policy matters to the tiniest particulars of office furniture. Excellence wasn't something superficial, imposed from above, but the tutelary spirit of a place, a reflection of the senior partner. As a man highly attuned to human psychology, Siegmund thought people betrayed themselves in minute ways. Lord Keynes would study people's hands as first clues to their characters, whereas Siegmund studied ties and developed numerous theories about them. (If you notice a man's tie, he once said, it's too loud.) On one occasion, in the heat of a takeover deal, he decided to drop a client when he noticed that the man wore monogrammed shirt cuffs—for Siegmund a sure tip-off of nouveau riche vanity. In this manner, Siegmund hewed to the old tradition of the private banker who studied his client's character as a clue to his business. We recall Pierpont Morgan's dictum that character was the basis of credit and that he wouldn't lend his money to a man he didn't trust for all the bonds in Christendom.

Having experienced firsthand the Great War, the hyperinflation of Weimar Germany, the 1931 banking crisis, and the Nazi seizure of power, Siegmund's personality had been molded by cataclysmic upheavals. This might have made somebody else fatalistic about trying to control events. Instead, it produced in Siegmund a wish to anticipate everything, then apply the most rigorous retrospective analysis to events that deviated from expectations. As part of this chess-master approach to business, two expressions were outlawed at the S.G. Warburg offices: "We'll cross that bridge when we come to it" and "There's no use crying over spilled milk." Siegmund thought you should first cross bridges in your imagination, and that spilled milk was the only kind worth crying over. With his insistence upon playing out takeover battles in advance in all their permutations, he became a virtually unbeatable force in the London world of mergers and acquisitions.

Knighted by Harold Wilson in 1966, Siegmund claimed legions of disciples who loved his passion and principle, his urbanity and erudition. There were also, it must be said, many people who found him pitiless, devious, and tyrannical. His conception of banking was similarly contradictory: a Janus-faced figure, he looked back to the origins of merchant banking and kept alive its best traditions while also pioneering many aspects of modern finance. Like the great private bankers of the early twentieth century, he saw himself as a high priest and physician, soul mate and confidant of his clients, privy to their innermost secrets; he wanted all-embracing relations with them, not just isolated transactions. He was the master of relationship banking because he peddled, not just financial knowledge, but class, charm, and learning. He once said that you couldn't become a man's banker until you first became his friend. To become Siegmund's client meant more than just concluding a single deal with him. It meant entering into his private world of literature, philosophy, politics, and psychology, not to mention his glittering social world of evenings at the opera and stimulating soirées at his Eaton Square home, capped by port and cigars. He may well have been the last great exponent of relationship banking.

At the same time, as a London transplant and newcomer, he had no choice but to buck the establishment and break all the rules. He had to wed the traditional banker's style to new functions, many of them anathema to the staid merchant banks. He needed to find a comparative advantage, one that required brains but not much capital, and he discovered it in merger work. During the famous Aluminium War of the late 1950s, he spearheaded the first hostile takeover of the modern era, shaking up forever his doddering rivals. Unlike the more prominent houses, he could violate the taboo against hostile takeovers because he didn't yet have the lengthy list of exclusive clients that made such a strategy dangerous; as we recall, the prestigious private banks had always refrained from such work for fear that one client might want to raid another. As a relative newcomer to London, Siegmund didn't have the establishmentarian's dread of making enemies. In 1963, he again innovated with an issue for the Autostrade Italiane—the Italian highway system—and helped to usher in the borderless world of the Euromarkets, rejuvenating London as a world financial center and restoring the free international capital flows he had known in the 1920s. Here he benefited from the insularity that afflicted the City of London during the interwar and early postwar years. With his extensive ties to German and continental bankers, Siegmund looked abroad at a time when his peers in the City still looked inward.

Yet he resisted certain advances. Having grown up with chronic uncertainty, he was pathologically averse to risk. Reflecting this, he didn't want his firm to trade securities, manage